Emotional Intelligence Mastery

The 30 Day Step by Step Practical Guide to Improving your EQ, Building Social Skills and Taking Your Life to The Next Level

By Gary Clyne

Table of Contents

Introduction

IQ is the main measurement of how intelligent a person is; however it is far from objective. While you can tell with a certain degree whether someone is smart based on their IQ, we cannot use it to measure how well they will perform. In fact, an employer looks for someone who is open-minded, willing to learn, and basically be decent enough to perform their jobs well alongside others. IQ does not tell that. A smart person can be arrogant and overall unpleasant, so they are detrimental to the organization. We should, instead, look at a person's emotional intelligence.

If you are reading this book, chances are that you are looking to improve. Then congratulations, you have taken the first step in improving your EQ because you need to recognize that you can improve yourself before you even begin. This book shall serve as a guide to help you become more successful by being a better parent, coworker, lover, friend, leader, and person.

Understanding Emotional Intelligence

Several sources suggest that emotional intelligence is basically the ability to monitor your own emotions and that of others. Moreover, EI also governs the ability to distinguish emotions and label them correctly. Most importantly, though, EI is the ability to use emotional intelligence as a guide for thoughts and behavior, as well as influence that of others. An alternate name for EI is Emotional Quotient (EQ for short).

We use EI when we empathize with others, have deep conversations about relationships, or attempt to manage a difficult individual. EI serves as a bridge to connect with others just as well as with ourselves, therefore making it key to a better life.

Although there are many kinds of interconnected intelligence, there are significant differences between them, one of which is IQ.

EQ vs. IQ

While EQ leans toward the emotional aspects, IQ is our cognitive intelligence. We are most familiar with IQ because it is often referred to whenever we need to measure someone's intelligence. Moreover, IQ is most often measured through tests, GPA, etc. IQ is the easiest to measure.

EI vs. SI

Social intelligence, SI for short, is more related to EI than IQ because SI is also crucial for the navigation of social or emotional situations. Still, they are two different types of intelligence even though they share similar features.

Emotional intelligence is more related to the present, meaning that it is used to identify, manage, and influence emotions in the moment. Social intelligence, on the other hand, focuses more on the future. It is basically understanding feelings, personalities, and behaviors of yourself and others to find positive outcomes.

EI in Psychology

Emotional intelligence served as a bridge in the mainstream understanding of intelligence, especially for psychologists. Psychology has always recognized that IQ is not everything, but failed to identify the missing piece in the past. Moreover, the components of this missing piece were even more elusive, as many could not agree on a single concept or ideas. They varied greatly. However, after the concept of emotional intelligence was introduced, psychologists found that it is the missing piece they were looking for.

Brief History of EI

To understand and embrace emotional intelligence, we need to understand where it came from. Let us start with the work of Peter Salovey.

Peter Salovey

Along with his colleague John Mayer, Peter Salovey produced the first formal theories of EI back in 1990. They coined the term emotional intelligence and defined it as "the ability to recognize, understand, utilize, and regulate emotions effectively in everyday life."

Thanks to their work, there was a spike in the interest in the subject both in the general public and in the academic fields. Judging by the proliferation of studies, research questions, and studies centering on emotional intelligence, we can safely conclude that the work of Salovey and Mayer has struck a chord with their theory of emotional intelligence, ultimately setting the foundation upon which further studies on the subject can be conducted.

Daniel Goleman

Soon after Salovey and Mayer brought EI to the world, many other researchers and psychologists started picking it up and running with it. Daniel Goleman was among the curious yet eager scholars, for he publishes the national bestselling book Emotional Intelligence in 1995 that helped ease the theories of EI into the mainstream.

According to Goleman, EI is vital to success, especially for children. He proposed that promoting their social and emotional learning to help boost their EI would improve their learning capabilities, and reduce or eliminate problematic, distracting, or detrimental behavioral problems in children, which greatly increase their chance of succeeding in school.

Thanks to his theories, the general public and research community alike have arrived at the conclusion that EI is just as important (if not more important) than IQ for individual success. The idea itself was welcomed and almost taken for granted to the point that it is almost common sense that your attitude defines your success, not ability. Plus, schools, educators, and education researchers have also welcomed the idea that EI is not something genetic. EI is a set of skills that one can learn and improve upon. It is not a trait that one simply is born with.

Travis Bradberry

After the groundbreaking book by Goleman, Travis Bradberry and Jon Greaves quickly capitalized on the growing interest on EI. Thus, Emotional Intelligence 2.0 was born that outlines a step-by-step program to enhance EI. Bradberry and Greaves propose 66 evidence-backed strategies to build and reinforce EI by teaching self-awareness, self-management, social awareness, and relationship management, all of which we will get to in a later chapter.

The book is so successful that even Dalai Lama, the famed Tibetan monk, claimed that it can assist you in comprehending the idea of EI, therefore opening a way for you to understand your own emotions and that of others. He also said that the book also offers a pre- and post-test to prove it.

Other Research and Studies on EI

There are countless studies out there on EI, its causes, associations, as well as consequences. However, we would like to bring your attention to three relatively recent ones that have garnered remarkable attention.

Lynda Jiwen Song and Colleagues

Back in 2010, they explored how EI and cognitive intelligence could influence college students' academic performance as well as social interactions. They have discovered that, while IQ is a good predictor of academic success, EQ contributes to this success in its own way. Moreover, the quality of social interactions with peers is greatly dependent on EQ rather than IQ, suggesting the latter has little use in students' social lives.

Kimmy S. Kee, Peter Salovey, and Colleagues

Back in 2009, they had an intriguing question about EQ and mental illness. Basically, they wondered if people with schizophrenia have lower EQ than those without mental illness. Schizophrenia is a mental disorder involving a breakdown in the relation between thoughts, emotions, and behavior, causing faulty perception, inappropriate actions and feelings, withdrawal from reality and personal relationships into fantasy and delusion, and a sense of mental fragmentation. As you might have guessed, Kimmy S. Kee and co. found that people with schizophrenia do have significantly lower EQ. Subjects were reported to have performed poorly on three out of four EQ tests that involved identifying, understanding, and managing emotions. Their poor performance can be associated with schizophrenia symptoms.

Delphine Nelis and Colleagues

Delphine and co. asked one of the most important questions about EI. The title of their paper "Increasing emotional intelligence: Is it possible?" already gives you an idea of what they worked on. Here, they created an experiment in which two groups were tested for their EQ. Subjects were tested at the beginning and at the end of the study. The treatment group received training called "brief empirically-derived EI training" which consists of four group training sessions for two and a half hours. Another (control) group received no such training. At the end of the experiment, the group that underwent training showed significant growth in EQ, whereas the other showed no growth at all.

All of these studies have answered some of the most important questions about EI and paved the way for more important and innovative works. We can say with certainty that EI is a vital factor success and it is just as critical in how we can relate to one another. We also know that our mental health plays an important role in EI. Most importantly, though, we know that we can actually improve our EI. It has been proven that EI is not a trait handed down through genes, although it is possible that it is where we receive a baseline level of EQ.

Emotional Intelligence Framework

To help you understand and remember what EI is all about, remember these two numbers: 5 and 4. Basically, there are 5 components of the EImodel and 4 dimensions.

5 Components of the EI Model

Daniel Goleman stated that there are five components (or elements) of EI. They are self-awareness, self-regulation, motivation, empathy, and social skills.

Self-Awareness

It can be defined as the ability to recognize and understand your own emotions. Self-awareness is the foundation of emotional intelligence because we need to understand and recognize our own emotions first before we can do the same to others.

Self-Regulation

When we are finally able to recognize our own emotions, the next logical step would be to regulate, and manage those emotions so we can appropriately express them.

Motivation

Those who score high in EI also have high intrinsic motivation. Basically, those with high EI can motivate themselves with internal reasons other than external rewards such as fame, wealth, respect, etc. These people have their own reasons to remain motivated and continue to work toward their own goals.

Empathy

To put it simply, empathy is the ability to feel what others feel. It does not mean sympathize, validate, or acceptance. It is the understanding of how others feel and recognizing how you would feel in their shoes on an intimate level.

Social Skills

Being the last piece of EI, these socials kills enable us to interact with others socially and navigate social situations successfully. People with high EI normally have higher-than-average socials kills and can pursue their goals effectively, which results in them achieving the outcomes that they want when they interact with others.

Organizational Context

The framework has been adapted and molded in order to fit business and organizational contexts. Here, there are a few sub-skills under each element that contribute to higher EI and success rate as a group member, employee, and organization member.

For self-awareness, there are three skills you can work on. The first is emotional awareness, which is the ability to recognize your emotions and their effects. Then, you need to be able to accurately self-assess by knowing your strengths and limits. Finally, you need to have self-confidence, which is defined as the sureness about your worth and capabilities.

For self-regulation, there are four skills. The first is self-control, which is the ability to manage your own disruptive emotions and impulses. Trustworthiness is the second on the list, and you simply need to maintain your standards of honesty and integrity. Conscientiousness is also another component of self-regulation, which involves taking responsibility for personal performance. Adaptability is the ability to be flexible in order to work around changes. Finally, innovativeness is basically being comfortable with new ideas or information, and open to them.

For self-motivation, there are four components. The first is the achievement drive, which means the ability to strive to improve or meet a standard of excellence. You will also need commitment which aligns with the goals of the organization or the group. The initiative is also crucial, which governs the readiness to act immediately on opportunities. Finally, optimism, characterized by the persistence in pursuing goals despite obstacles and setbacks.

For empathy, you need to be able to sense others' feelings and perspective, as well as taking an active interest in their concerns. Empathy also includes service orientation, meaning that you need to anticipate, recognize, and meet the needs of customers. Empathy also involves developing others by knowing what they need and help them bolster their abilities. Leveraging diversity is also another component in empathy and it is basically the cultivation of opportunities through diverse people. Finally, political awareness, which is the ability to read a group's emotional currents and power relationships.

Finally, for social skills, you need to focus on eight elements. The first is the influence, which means the ability to wield and utilize effective tactics for persuasion. Next is communication, which requires you to send clear and convincing messages. Leadership involves inspiring and guiding groups of people. You might also need to be the change catalyst, which means you need to initiate and manage change. Meanwhile, you need to manage conflicts through the negotiation and resolution of disagreements. Building bonds is also important because you need to nurture instrumental relationships. Of course, collaboration and cooperation is also a vital component of social skills. Finally, you need to understand your group's capabilities because success depends on the creation of group synergy in pursuing collective goals.

4 Dimensions of EI

According to Salovey and Mayer, there are four branches or dimensions of EI that create a hierarchy of emotional skills and abilities. They are perceiving emotion, using emotions to facilitate thoughts, understanding emotions, and managing emotions.

Perceiving Emotions

The first branch relates to being aware and recognize other people's conditions. Here, you need to understand their physical and psychological conditions such as having a headache or feeling dizzy. Moreover, it also governs identifying emotions in other people, expressing your one emotions and needs clearly and accurately. Plus, it also relates to being able to distinguish between accurate and honest feelings from inaccurate and dishonest feelings.

Using Emotions to Facilitate Thoughts

It involves taking advantage of your own mood swings so you can appreciate multiple points of views, generating emotions to facilitate your judgment and memory better, redirecting and prioritizing your thinking based on your feelings linked to those thoughts, and using your own emotional states to boost your problem-solving skills and creativity.

Understanding Emotions

The third branch of EI involves understanding the interconnection among emotions, understanding and perceiving the causes, and consequences of, and transitions between emotions, as well as understanding complex feelings and contradictory states.

Managing Emotions

Finally, managing emotions involves being open to all emotions, no matter how pleasant or unpleasant they are. It also involves engaging, prolonging, or detaching from an emotional state, monitoring and reflecting on your emotions, as well as managing that within yourself and in others.

Traits vs. State

We used the word "condition" in the previous section. Conditions or states refer to the temporary thought patterns, behaviors, and feelings that vary greatly depending on the current circumstance as well as the individual's personality. On the other hand, trait refers to the permanent or semi-permanent thought patterns, behaviors, and feelings that remain consistent, long-lasting, and stable despite the ever-changing present circumstance.

We can say that EI leans toward the "trait" part on the trait-state scale, even though our EI and related skills and abilities are dependent on the current circumstance. For example, you can display a higher level of EI in personal relationships compared to work situations, or vice versa. Still, EI is not usually considered to be a trait.

High and Low EI

Although EQ tests are not widely used as IQ tests, you do not need to fetch that exam paper and have someone do it to know whether someone has high or low emotional intelligence. You can tell if someone has high or low EI based on their behavior.

High EQ

There are 6 main qualities that you need to look for in individuals who have high EQ.

First, they understand that change is a fact of life, so they are quick to adapt to such changes, which makes them more open to change.

Second, they know well what they are good at, what they can work on, and what kind of environment suits them the best. This self-awareness is critical because it is impossible to know where you go wrong if you do not know what you get right first. With that knowledge, they embrace their strengths and weaknesses and compensate for the latter by leveraging the former.

Third, people with EQ tend to display a high level of empathy toward others. This allows high EQ individuals to connect with others on a personal level, strengthening trust and bond and reinforcing the group's synergy.

Fourth, they understand that no work is insignificant if they put enough care and attention into doing it. They value high-quality work and they have a sharp focus, not letting themselves be distracted easily.

Still, they understand that perfection is merely an ideal, an impossibility.

Fifth, they have a healthy work-life balance. While this may seem that the individual simply has a happy life by knowing when to work and when to play, maintaining that balance also stop people from becoming too negligent, informal, or otherwise be too goal-oriented in the workplace. Having a healthy work-life balance allow individuals to be easy-going while focusing on how to move forward without holding onto grudges. They are gracious, happy, and grateful.

Sixth, individuals with high EQ remain open-minded at all times, accepting new ideas and are always eager to explore new possibilities. However, they may be a bit guarded because they understand when to open up and when to stick to their boundaries.

Low EQ

There are also some good signs of low EQ, other than the opposite of the six we just mentioned.

First, individuals who have low EQ have difficulty in controlling their own emotions. At the same time, they are clueless about the feelings of others, even those who are close to them. As such, they cannot maintain good personal or work relationships. This inability to be sympathetic with others could lead very quickly to sadness and crippling depression, with which they too find it hard to cope.

In many social situations, they are likely to put on the expressionless "poker face", which makes it hard for others to read them. On the inside, they are often emotionally inappropriate for the occasion. During conversations, they are emotionally "tone deaf", which means that they have trouble reading emotions from other's tone of voice.

A good way to tell if someone lacks EQ is to see how they react to emotional events. If they remain unmoved by emotional scenes in movies, books, or TV series no matter the genre, or they are unaware of their own dog's emotion state even when the signs are clear, then you can say with certainty that they lack EQ.

Sometimes, a person with low EQ may overstate the importance of logic over emotions. Of course, this might not apply to everyone, even though it is logically sound to make judgments based on logic and not emotions. Individuals with low EQ may outright trivialize the importance of emotions as a whole.

Why Developing EI is Crucial

Okay, that is quite enough theory crafting. The big question is why you should even bother working on your EI skills when you have a paper due this Monday. Okay, fair enough. Finish that paper first if you must. But you need to work on your EI skills, especially if you display some of the characteristics of low EQ above.

Why? Because the importance of being able to understand your own emotions can never be overstated. It is fundamental to understand the things that allow you to perform better and have a better life as a whole. We are, as humans, highly social and emotional creatures after all. Being intelligent emotionally allow you to connect with others on a personal level, not to mention that you can boost your performance at work, improve your communication skills, and allow you to be more resilient to the unforgiving world. Having a high level of EI allows you to be more successful in just about any aspect of your life.

EI for Therapists, Educators, etc.

If you work as a coach, therapist, counselor, educator, or any other positive psychology-related role, then you might already know the importance of high EI. Basically, when you can understand, recognize, and manage both positive and negative emotions in your clients, improving your interactions with them and increasing your success rate.

Without EI, you will soon find that your interventions are ineffective because if the people you work with cannot "read" you, then they might not trust you as much. If they do not get a real-life example of emotional intelligence, they will have a hard time working on it as well.

Self and Relationship Management

Self-management and relationship-management are the two critical skills to have in life if you want to get far. Not only do they help us lead healthier, happier lives, they also help us get through our daily lives, no matter how rough they are.

The first step is, of course, self-management, because we need to learn how to manage ourselves first before we can cultivate healthy, meaningful relationships with others. Learning self-management allows you to manage your own emotions and motivate yourself in most situations. Then, your relationship management skills allow you to build healthy, meaningful relationships as well as communicate effectively by being open with others, persuading others of your views, and being honest without offending or alienating others.

Having a higher EQ really help in improving these two skills, as with many others. For example, if you have high EQ, then you will be a good employer, manager, or business owner. Thanks to its versatility, EQ remains the most critical element to success.

EI in the Workplace

An organization's success relies heavily on its workers. Only when the members are highly emotionally intelligent can they work in unison to achieve maximum productivity. This is the only way to achieve long-term success. EI can do wonders for any organizations because its use allows you to understand how relationships and people function. Workers with high EQ will show their excellence in leadership, partnership, teamwork, and vision consistently because they know clearly about their relationship with the staff, organizations, customers, directors, networking contacts, competitors, etc.

On a broader scale, organizations with higher EQ take in staff that is productive, motivated, efficient, effective, likable, and have common goals. As mentioned earlier, EQ is very versatile and it is applicable to every human interaction in any circumstances, especially in business. Having high EQ allows the organization to provide better customer service, coming up with better ideas and solutions, and many other activities.

On a more personal level, having high EI allows you to better assess people better, understand how relationships develop, how beliefs generate, and how to use our experience to prevent power struggles, resistance, negativity in the workplace, etc. to increase vision and success.

EI and Decision-Making

This should not come as a surprise, but high EQ results in better decision-making. When you understand yourself and others clearly, you can weigh all options properly by having an open mind and muting all other irrelevant emotions (not ALL emotions) from the decision-making process. By removing emotions that can affect their decision-making, especially those that can interfere such as anxiety, you can stay more objective while still using your gut feelings to a healthy extent.

EI and Communication

Building upon the previous section, EI is closely related to communication skills as well. People who are proficient in their communication abilities often have high EQ. They may display certain traits such as the fact that they consider other people's feelings and that of their own by practicing empathy for others and trying to relate to them during conversations. Moreover, those people operate on trust by building it through verbal and nonverbal cues and honest communication. As such, high EI results in better, healthier, and more competent connections, which is required for a healthy professional and personal life.

EI and Relationships

On a more personal level, EI can be used to foster and maintain healthy relationships. It is not hard to see how high EQ can mean better relationships for you.

Those with high EQ can read other people's emotions and react to them appropriately. They can understand and regulate their own emotions so they do not let negative things affect them too much, if at all. They do not bottle things up and understand that their thoughts create their own emotions. As such, they can take control of their own thoughts and actions accordingly.

Because of this, it is no wonder why people high in EI have more stable, satisfying and healthier relationships than others. All of their interactions are done very carefully so as not to cause any unintended negativity to both themselves and others, making them very likable.

Nursing and Healthcare

EI has a special place in these two fields for very good reasons. Nurses, for instance, do not experience burnout as often while maintaining good mental and physical health in addition to performing well, if they have high EI.

Nurses or other healthcare professionals will have an easier time working if they can identify emotions in themselves and that of others accurately to administer proper care. Not only that, but high EI also enables them to reason with their patients a lot better, not to mention being able to trust their gut feelings while working in conjunction with objective reasoning. All of the above add up to a very effective healthcare professional.

Resilience and EI

EI also plays a huge role in our resilience. Those who are high in EI are usually better at recovering after they fail. In reality, EI is considered by many to be a direct source of resilience. According to Magnano, Craparo, and Paolillo, EI is directly linked to resilience. Only through resilience can people achieve and motivate themselves to achieve.

Basically, those who have high EI are more successful because they work harder than others for it, and they recover and move on quickly when they fail. As stated earlier, we can work on our EI. With the theory crafting out of the way, let us get into the more exciting part of the book, the action part.

The Application of Emotional Intelligence

EI has many uses, especially when it comes to handling impulses, difficulties, setbacks, pressure, and anxiety.

Handling Impulses

Improving impulse control is where many people struggle as they get older, not to mention that the practice itself is not that easy. Still, handling impulses is critical in dealing with issues such as procrastination, addiction, and productivity.

Just like EQ, impulse control is a learned behavior. While it may seem easy for you to stop yourself from acting on something you want immediately even if the consequences are very detrimental, the skill itself takes years to develop. Thanks to technology and how interconnected the world is, stopping yourself from doing negative things can be harder than it looks. A lot of things are very easy now. You have fast food that can be served in minutes, instant payment, and immediate gratification from social media and video games, instant celebrity on social media or reality TV, and even drugs and medication.

When it comes to impulse control, there are two stages you need to overcome. First, you need to be able to stop yourself and think things through. Then, you need to maintain the resistance after the pause. Failing in doing one of these will have you acting on your impulse that can be detrimental to your life. It is a sad reality that many of us want the easy way out. We tend to choose easy and quick solutions over the difficult ones, even if the latter is more valuable. If you can control that impulse to take the easy way out and evaluate all the benefits you can get just by putting in the extra efforts. So, how do you control your impulse?

Interrupt the Impulse

First, start by setting up conditions to delay your acting on impulses immediately. You can control your own impulse better if the temptation is not there and that you need to take extra effort to satisfy. Here are some examples:

- Lock up the video games consoles or delete video games from your computer
- Throw away the cigarettes

- Remove snacks from your house if you go on a diet
- Delete bookmarks from your web browser
- Unplug the TV or put the remote in a hard-to-reach location
- Drive a different route to bypass the tempting stores you want to stop

As mentioned earlier, this works because you need to do a few things before you can get that satisfaction. While we live in a world where we expect to get things easy and quick, you can use this to your advantage. Many people would not even bother watching TV if they have to grab the remote somewhere hard to find, like under the cushion. By putting additional steps to satisfy your impulse, you can easily dismiss it with a quick "It's not worth it,"

Maintaining Control

Next, you need to figure out a way to maintain that control. While the initial impulse can be suppressed, you need to keep it down and this is, if not harder, just as hard as the first step. For some people, fighting off impulse is a difficult thing, especially for those who have addictions. They are willing to go the extra mile just to satisfy their impulse. Interrupting yourself at this stage is much more complex, but there are some ways to do this.

Sometimes, you have a hard time fighting off temptation because you do not have much else to do at the moment. So, the solution would be to substitute it for a healthier and more immediate reward treat. For example, if you are trying to cut down on drinking, maybe put a dollar into your vacation saving every time you managed to resist the urge. Alternatively, make a bet with yourself or with others that you can resist the temptation for a period of time and reach your goal.

You can also satisfy your own urge in a controlled manner. For example, you can limit your dessert to one time each week. However, we do not recommend you do this because, while doing this can keep the urge from becoming too strong that could lead you on to an uncontrollable binge, it could also weaken your resolve and actually makes it hard for you to suppress your urge next time it happens.

Other people have reported that by leaving notes to themselves, they can remind themselves constantly to not give in to temptation. So, try leaving notes with reasons to maintain the resistance. If you are trying to maintain a diet, put up notes reminding yourself of the health benefits of healthy eating on the fridge or cupboard. If you are trying to quit smoking, put up notes detailing why you shouldn't in your pocket or wherever you usually keep your cigarettes. If you are trying to cut down on your spending, try wrapping up your credit card in a piece of paper with a note to yourself to stop spending money on the things you don't really need. There is also an old internet joke where people keep a picture of Terry Crews (wearing a dark shirt, looking really disappointed/angry at you) in their wallet. They do this to remind themselves of how disappointed Terry Crews would be if they spend money on the things you don't need. While doing this can be a bit of a stretch, everyone can get a laugh at it whenever you open up your wallet. Try it out!

Another way to suppress the urge is by imagining the dark side of it. For example, you can have a better time not drinking for the night if you think of how hangover you would be the next morning. For drug addiction, well, everyone knows how lives can be ruined with them so think about that as well. If you are on a diet, think of how much fatter you would be if you eat that bag of chips. Think of all the cute clothing that you cannot fit into because of your shape. Or, think of how the food will do to the body. The cholesterol will interrupt the blood flowing into your heart, not to mention many other diseases. Think of all the fun things you could miss if you fall ill because you do not eat healthy now. If you are trying to stop yourself from watching TV or playing video games, think of how much time lost. Take a step back and look at yourself from a third-person perspective and observe how much more you could have done if you do not just sit there all day, letting time breeze by for nothing.

Handling Difficulties and Setbacks

One of the things that we all need to accept is the fact that everyone will face difficulties in life. Everyone has different problems, and yours is probably not as bad compared to others. Many have endured many harsh situations and came through. So, you can always remember that you will come out of the other side just fine. Remembering this is important because we will all face setbacks in our life now and again, both in our personal relationships or in our careers. However, people deal with setbacks differently. Some are good, many are bad at it. So, what is the difference?

Types of Obstacles

Although defeats, roadblocks, and setbacks are all classified as obstacles standing between where you are now and where you want to be, each one of them is a different level of challenge.

The first and smallest obstacle is setbacks. They are minor hiccups, inconveniences, really. They just slow you down and makes it a bit harder to progress or less likely to succeed. A good example would be if you have a project and you want to start working on it on Monday. However, let's say that your PC broke down so you could not start until Wednesday. It is not a big deal, but it does force you to hurry things up a bit to make it in time.

The second kind of obstacle is roadblocks. These do more harm than slowing you down. Think of them as tar papers. They are threats that can make you stuck. They impede your progress and prevents you from accomplishing something. For instance, suppose that you want to complete the project by Friday, but your file got corrupted and you cannot finish it until Monday, making you miss your deadline and upsetting your boss or client to the point that you are not even sure if you can right the wrong. Even if you can keep your job or client, you might feel the sting from that event. If it is a client, they might not go to you as often and you become the second if not last, choice. If it is your boss, then they might give you less important work because they simply cannot trust you. Here, you can always bounce back but it will take a lot of time and effort.

Finally, the third type of obstacles is defeats. These are the most crushing of them all. They can change your life and even make you question it. You may need to do a complete 180 turn in the process if you need to cope with this obstacle. For example, suppose that you are very hyped up for the promotion you were promised but was given to someone else last minute. You were really hoping for it, but your expectations are crushed. Worse, you have been working hard for that company for years, only to be told rather coldly that you are being let go. These kinds of obstacles are not those tiny jabs that sting, but you can brush off, or the kinds that knock you down only to motivate you to try harder. These kinds of obstacles will knock you down, kick you while you're down, and make sure you stay down. This is where people go wrong in coping and ultimately ruin their lives. Thankfully, you can always pick yourself up and move on. Before we talk about the right way to respond, let us look at how your "normal" response is not a good one.

People often cast blames everywhere but themselves when they have problems with career or relationships. They have a hundred reasons that put them where they are that are completely out of their control. If that is you, then you might have told someone that you lost the job because your boss was a jerk or that you would not have lost that promotion had your PC not broken down so conveniently.

Another natural response to setbacks, roadblocks, or defeats is anger. It feels like whatever happened to you is unjust and that you are wrongly punished. You might also feel sad or frustrated because you let yourself and others down, or because you feel that you are not where you want to be in your life. You might also be scared of what lies ahead depending on the size of the problem. While all of these responses are natural, these might hurt yourself more. How?

It is very understandable that you would feel frustrated, angry, sad, or scared when you are dealing with obstacles. However, they present a huge problem.

None of these responses will get you anywhere. Worse still, they can stop you right in your track.

According to a study back in 2010 by the University of Miami, depressed people who cannot get over the obstacles in their lives are more likely to think about it all the time. They eventually allow themselves to be caught in their own despair, no matter how serious or insignificant the problem really is. They continue to dwell on it all the time, which drains their energy while not helping their case at all. If that is you, then there is something important to remember.

Setbacks Are Inevitable

Everyone will have to endure setbacks, even successful people. Everyone has faced their fair share of problems before, during, and after achieving something amazing. Take Steve Jobs, for example. He co-founded Apple when he was 21 and went on to become a millionaire within two years. He was removed from his position from Apple just a few years later after he had a disagreement with the company's co-founder. This act is equivalent to firing, and to be fired from the company you helped create is a painful event indeed.

This led Jobs to a midlife crisis. However, he remained unfazed and thought carefully about his other career options, which led him to create NeXT and Pixar, which are pretty successful, before he returned to Apple that was floundering after he left. So, even when he was jobless, he managed to turn things around and led Apple to its prominent position today.

The point is that you can overcome whatever obstacles are in your way, and you can reach that better place. All you really need is to develop the right strategies. Here, psychologists have identified three ways of coping:

Problem-focused coping involves solving problems by taking steps to remove threats one at a time and find solutions. If you use this approach, you can narrow your attention down to the smaller problems at hand, allowing you to focus on what really matters and not let competing activities get in the way. Another great thing about problem-focused coping is the fact that you will face your fear and look at it in the eyes, studying it until you break it down to its base elements. By then, the problem seems a lot less scary because you have already drained it of its debilitating power. Besides, you will need to solve the problems eventually, so it helps if you can see what needs to be dealt with in advance.

Another coping mechanism is known as emotion-focused coping, which involves managing your own emotions. Sometimes, we need sympathy from others and talk about how we feel about doing something. This kind of coping normally involves talking through experiences with others who love and care about you. Think of it as molding a piece of clay. It all started with a huge clump and, as the conversation goes on, it starts to take shape that transforms the meaning that we make about our experience. Just by talking alone, you can allocate blame and praise more objectively. You can also gain new perspectives, correct problematic ones, and find new insights.

Finally, avoidance is also a coping mechanism. Though it rarely works, it involves not talking or thinking about it and hopes it goes away. Here, people shut out their feelings related to the problem. Here is where people turn to drugs or alcohol, but they are not the only way. People find other ways to disengage from their feelings or distract themselves. Again, this is not recommended but it can be helpful sometimes, especially if you do not want to deal with the problem until you are ready psychologically to confront that traumatic experience. But if you continue to avoid, problems will begin to pile up.

The best way to cope with a problem is the first one, but you might need to use the second one to motivate yourself through, and the third one is useful when you need to mentally prepare yourself. Still, there are a few things worth pointing out before you start taking action.

There Are No Straight Lines

Unfortunately, many things in life are not simple or straightforward. The same applies when overcoming adversity or dealing with it. It is not a linear progression. Going in a straight line means stasis. Solving problems involves a lot of ups and downs. You need both the dips and peaks to keep moving forward. That much is clear. The peaks remind you where you want to be, whereas the dips motivate you to reach for the sky. Eventually, the ups will push you higher and the downs are not as bad. Basically, as long as you keep moving forward, you will soon notice the improvement in the long run.

Now, you might be wondering how exactly you are supposed to do to get over what happened to you. As always, you need a plan to overcome adversaries. This involves using the first coping mechanism – problem-focused coping. Your plan must include effective strategies so you can actually go somewhere. Start by setting a SMART goal. Basically, the goal needs to be Specific, Measurable, Attainable, Reasonable, and Time-bound. Make it crystal clear of what you want, create a way to measure your progress, make sure the goal is actually possible and within reasonable reach, and have a serious deadline. Then, there are five more things you can do right now to help you overcome your obstacles so you can emerge victorious on the other side to tell the tale.

Give Yourself Time

The first things you need to do is to give yourself some time to process what happened. Too many times have people let their emotions get the best of them in the heat of the moment, leading them to make rash and irrational decisions that they later come to regret. Instead, sit down, have a glass of cool water to cool yourself down, and let your mind absorb what happened and analyze where you are right now. Most of the time, you do not need to respond to the problem immediately, and no one should expect that from you either. It is always better to take some time to think things through before you decide on your next move. The amount of time you should give yourself depends on the weight of the situation. If it is something big, give yourself a full day to let it out if you must. Again, allocate enough time until you can calm down. Whatever amount of time you choose, make sure you stick to it. Take as much time as you need to come to terms with what has happened, and then figure out how to proceed from there.

Do Not Panic

It is becoming rather old nowadays to see people in movies panicking only to make matters worse. Take the first American astronaut to orbit Earth, John Glenn, for example. He spent an entire day in space monitoring his heart rate, making sure it never went over 100 beats a minute. You want to have that kind of control over your emotions when you are facing a setback. While you spend some alone time to adjust to the new situation, never allow yourself to panic. That will not help anyone at all. If anything, it hurts more than it helps.

Accept Failures

When someone tells you not to think of a blue elephant, the first thing that comes to your mind is the blue elephant. The same thing applies to the fear of failure. If you are afraid of failing, you might actually increase your chance of failing. Instead, make peace with failure so you do not need to worry about reaching your potential. Basically, realize that the situation is what it is, accept it, and move on.

Take babies, for example. What would happen if babies never get up after falling once when they try to walk? What would our world be like? How do you want to live the rest of your life? Are you going to let a few failures get in the way of achieving something truly meaningful? Of course not. While you cannot change what has happened, you can choose to either deal with it or let it define you.

Another way to look at failure is by asking yourself "What's the worst that could happen?" Okay, that sounds like one of the famous final words in horror movies, but really. What is the worst that could happen to you? If you cannot get that job, then you will remain jobless and you can always apply for another one. If you do not get promoted, then you will still get to keep your job, and you can still try harder next time. If your lover dumped you, then you will have more opportunities to get to know many other interesting people. We do not really fear failure as much as we are led to believe. We are actually afraid of the unknown. That is why we keep asking ourselves "What if I fail?" So, by actually confronting your fears and analyze what could possibly happen should you fail, you basically eliminate your fear of failure. Again, you are not really afraid of failing. You are afraid because you do not know what would happen if you fail. When you know that the worst thing that could happen is not that bad, you will have a lot easier time to embrace failure should it happen to you. You can move forward easier.

Cut Yourself Some Slack

Another thing worth mentioning is that you should not beat yourself up too harshly over what has happened. While it may be no one's fault but your own, there is no point in dwelling on it any longer than you should. As mentioned earlier, failure is inevitable, and to err is human. The world is already unforgiving as it is. The best thing you can do is being more forgiving on yourself. Sure, you could have written that report better or worked harder, but at least you know what you need to do to get better. Give yourself an encouraging pat on the back, move on, and try harder. If you are too harsh on yourself, you are actually telling yourself that you are not good enough for the position, which only sets you up for more failures down the road.

Regain Control

Finally, you need to take back as much control over the situation as possible so to prevent yourself from feeling hopeless and helpless. This involves considering the actions you need to take to help you overcome your obstacles. For instance, if you are called into your boss's office because you produced a report of questionable quality, ask yourself (or the boss directly) what you can do to prevent this from happening. Maybe you need more time to work on it. Maybe you need more tools at your disposal. It is easy to overthink here, but try to limit your thoughts to the things that you can actually control. When you have identified what you can change, you will feel more in control.

Handling Stress and Anxiety

Stress and anxiety are two of the biggest problems you need to deal, especially in the workplace. That is hardly fair, considering that you already need to spend 8 hours sitting in an office, and now you need to deal with the problems in your head. Stress and anxiety can drastically affect your overall quality of life and you will eventually feel that your life is nothing but numbers. The number of hours you need to work, when to start, when to stop, how much you earn, deadlines, etc. It is so bleak, is it not? About three-quarters of people in the world with stress or anxiety in their life say that these two mental problems affect their daily lives. The workplace is no exception, either. Anxiety can have a negative impact on your productivity and your relationships. If you have been diagnosed with an anxiety disorder, then things will be a lot harder for you.

In the Workplace

Deadlines and difficult people are the biggest sources of stress in the workplace. Conflict in the workplace will expose you to drama and a good dose of stress as well. Though some people love drama, others would rather walk out of the room if they can until the commotion passes. Regardless, the problem is probably the lack of effective communication. This can lead to a good amount of anxiety. When a lot of people in the workplace are affected by anxiety, you can almost feel the stress coming from them. That stress is also contagious. By then, people will begin to miss more work and the quality goes down. Things will start to be very visible when coworkers start gossiping and whine rather than working together to solve the problem. Eventually, people will stop talking to each other, accumulating a mountain of grievances, making the workplace outright toxic. That is not a place you want to work in.

So, the first logical step would be to create a personal wellness plan. If you get enough sleep, healthy food, exercise, and socializing, then you are well on your way to reduce stress and anxiety. Even if you have all the above, reducing stress and anxiety is more complicated than that. You also need to observe how you function in the workplace system and how you deal with others. That is why self-awareness is the first on the list of EI components. Do you wait to speak up until you are bursting into tears or seething with anger? Do you gossip? Do you hide from your boss? These are the things you should notice when you are working. From there, you can implement a few strategies to help make the workplace calmer and less toxic so you can come home with a clearer mind.

Know Everyone's Name

Okay, no one expects you to remember well over ten names on the first day of work. Still, you need to maintain a solid personal relationship with people in the workplace so you can work with them to address problems better. When you know someone well, it is a lot easier to point out their flaws and have your ideas accepted. Without a solid relationship, all you can really do is gossip and vent to others. To have a solid relationship, you need to know their name. Again, no one expects you to remember well over ten names if you barely interact at all. Just say something like, "I'm terribly sorry, but I seem to have forgotten your name." and they will tell you again. There is no big deal about forgetting someone's name anyway. Remember that it is never too late to start building stronger relationships at the office.

Seek Assistance

When things get busy in the workplace, you might catch yourself saying "yes" when someone asks you to do something that you don't really understand. In some cases, you just do not want to say no. While asking for help might seem embarrassing, many people are actually willing to help you. All you need is reaching out. Plus, the discomfort of seeking assistance is worth it in the long run because you can learn something new, and you can reduce the overall anxiety about the work as a whole. Besides, asking for help is not a sign that you are incompetent. Not doing it properly is. Asking for help is actually a sign that you genuinely care about doing something right.

Set Honest Deadlines

Consider this an extension from the previous section. Sometimes, you agree to a deadline that you know you cannot meet, only to scramble everything last second and end up disappointing everyone. Instead, you should just be honest that you cannot do it on time rather than apologizing later. While not every deadline is negotiable, you will save yourself from hours of anxiety-induced moments if you are honest and work at a manageable pace. If you do, you might even finish the work ahead of time, which makes you look even better.

Avoid Triangles

A lot of workplaces are built on toxicity. It is all about gossiping and venting about others. This only provides temporary relief or entertainment, and not much else. In fact, it only builds up even more tension or stress. When the office is becoming toxic, you can almost smell it when you walk through the door. This is where the word "triangle" and "triangling" come in.

Basically, triangling means you bond with someone by talking about a third person. It works because you two have someone to hate in common, but it is an unhealthy way to manage anxiety. Triangles include gossiping, criticizing someone behind their back, or using them as a scapegoat.

While it might be tempting to vent out to a coworker about how difficult someone is, consider how you can limit the scale of the problem. Try to keep it between you and the person causing you problems. An alternative would be to meet up with that person in private and be open about it. Make sure that the other person understands that you are on their side and that you want to work with them to solve their problems to create an open and honest workplace. If you are a supervisor or an employer, think of the ways you can encourage employees to work out their differences and work together instead. Encourage them to approach you openly if they have a problem with your leadership. Basically, as a leader, try to praise in public and reprimand in private.

Use Neutral Language

Knowing how to use neutral and calming language in the office can help bring everyone's anxiety down during the work hours. Disagreements will be a lot calmer if you start your statement with something like "Here's what I think," and end it with, "What about you?" Doing so allows people to feel that they have a say in the matter, and participation is important when solving conflicts. Plus, when others feel that their opinions are also being considered, they open up easier to your ideas. Even when there are differences you need to overcome, everyone will be a lot more forgiving. Other questions such as "How could we prevent this from coming up in the future?" or "What could we do about this issue?" are great to solve problems as well, especially for leaders.

Stay in Contact

We often find it hard to remain in contact with people who are not as relevant in our lives, or those who make us feel uncomfortable. The same applies to the workplace. Perhaps you avoid the break room when you had a heated argument with a coworker. Maybe you stopped replying to emails that you do not know how to answer. Maybe you avoided your boss. The problem here is avoidance, and it will only make matters worse. Your anxiety will only get worse over time the more you use distance to cope with your problems.

Instead, maintain contact. In the workplace, contact is the bloodline of the organization. You need to work on it as often as possible to strengthen communication. When you work hard on maintaining good communication, many confrontations will be less anxiety-inducing and uncomfortable. Many great leaders can maintain contact with those who they do not agree with in terms of perspective or styles of work. Plus, by maintaining your contact, you can say "no" easier to additional responsibilities.

Do Not Drag Others Down

In the workplace, everyone expects each other to pull their own weight. That much is already clear by day one. Still, office drama often occurs and can make the environment more stressful. It also lowers morale, though drama is entertaining sometimes. So, what can you do? You can try to intervene and change the subject when people start talking poorly of other coworkers or the boss. If not, just find an excuse to walk out of the room. Bathroom break works. Moreover, when you receive texts or emails that are made to drag others down, do not respond to them.

Encourage In-Person Conversation

We are becoming too dependent on electronic communication that we forgot how valuable it really is. Think about it. It is actually very difficult to understand emotions and intentions in an email. When you have a one-on-one talk with someone, you can hear their tones, their body gestures, and their facial expressions, all of which help you understand what the other person really is trying to say. Besides, much of the workplace anxiety comes from misinterpreting emails or waiting to receive an email back about a difficult subject. If something makes you feel anxious, perhaps you should have a private conversation with that other person to clear things up.

Focus on Facts

In the heat of the moment, it is easy to lose your mind and let your emotions take over. So, to lower anxiety during stressful moments, try to control the conversation and what is communication. For example, try to say exactly what is causing you stress and anxiety, and ask others to share their views. Then, make sure you make it clear to everyone of how you want the problem to be solved (in most cases, peacefully). Focus on the facts in front of you and stay in the present. Arguing by bringing up the past problems is not going to help, no matter how relevant they seem.

Access Resources

Most of the time, your workplace offers counseling through employee assistance programs. That, or they offer to help you connect to mental health resources in the community to help you manage anxiety. While it can be intimidating to admit weakness and speak up about your anxiety, you are actually setting an example by taking responsibility for your wellness.

Mind, Body, and Action

Of course, stress and anxiety are not exclusive to the workplace. There will be a time when you feel them during social gatherings or other events as well. As such, you need to work on three areas (mind, body, and action) so you can maintain control of the situation.

Mind

First, start by accepting the fact that not everything is under your control. No one really is in charge of everything and no one knows everything. As mentioned earlier, you are not anxious about the worst. You are anxious about the unknown. As always, slow down and access the situation. Is it really as bad as you think? Instead of focusing on the things that you cannot control, try to improve the situation by doing what you can.

This leads us to the second point: do your best. No one expects you to do things perfectly because perfection is an ideal. Instead of aiming for perfection, be proud of what you have done. While it is not perfection, you know that you cannot do it any better. As such, you should strive to maintain a positive attitude. Make an effort to replace negative thoughts with positive ones. There are plenty of ways to do this. You can write down encouraging notes to yourself that you can consult when you feel down. You can feed yourself positive thoughts before you sleep and after you wake up. You can also hang up notes to remind yourself.

Finally, know what triggers your anxiety. Maybe it is work, school, family, or something else you can identify. Write it down when you feel stressed or anxious and try to find a pattern.

Body

There are plenty of things you can do to your body to reduce anxiety. Start by limiting alcohol and caffeine intake. We know that a cup of coffee in the morning is the best pick-me-up ever, but it also gives you the shakes. Alcohol after a long day at work is not recommended as well because it just makes you forget about the problem. Drink plain water instead.

Also, eat well-balanced meals. Skipping breakfast for coffee will not do your body any good. Eat meals three times a day, but make sure your intake is balanced. Also, try to keep some energy-boosting, healthy snacks ready with you just in case you need to munch on something.

Strive to get at least 7 hours of sleep a night. 8 hours is recommended, but when you are busy, just 7 will do. However, when you feel stressed, you will need more rest so try to get 8 hours of sleep every night.

Finally, exercise regularly. It makes you feel good and maintain your health. Try to do it every day. You do not have to visit the gym, either. There are many at-home exercises to be found on YouTube.

Action

Sometimes, you need to take action to control your anxiety. One of which is taking deep breaths. As mentioned earlier, it is easy to get caught in the heat of the moment and do things you regret later. Taking deep breaths help you slow down and access the situation better. While you are at it, you can also combine deep breaths with counting. Some people find counting up to 10 helps. So, you can try counting your breaths up to 10 when you are faced with a particularly difficult situation. If you need to, take some time to meditate, practice yoga, listen to music, get a message, or learn other relaxation techniques. Take a step back from your problems to clear your head first.

You can reduce anxiety and stress by back to your community. Volunteer or find another way to be active in your community, which creates a support network and gives you a break from everyday stress. At the same time, if you are struggling, you can always find help. Turning to your friends and family is ideal, but there are many support groups out there. You can take up a mental health screen, which is anonymous, free, and private. Still, there is hardly anything better than talking to your friends or family member when you feel overwhelmed. Remember that they are always ready to help you.

Coping with Trauma

If you have past trauma such as deaths, losses, violence or other assaults, you might find yourself reliving those memories and events from those past events. Common reactions include denial, shock, fatigue, moodiness, hypervigilance, guilt, feeling of helplessness, depression, numbness, social withdrawal, and many more. There are some reasons why you are struggling.

Death of a Loved One

Arguably the worst thing that could happen to you, such traumatic events often include injury or death of someone you love or care about. You might know someone who died during a tragic event. That or the event remind you of other deaths or losses. Such a traumatic event is not exclusive to the death of humans, though. Some people have reported feeling traumatized after the death of their pets.

Cumulative Trauma

We connect traumas psychologically. If you experience a new one before you have recovered from the past one, you may experience the separate events as related. This can lead to intensified symptoms and longer recovery time. When you experience cumulative traumatic incidents, you may feel a greater sense of disconnectedness from yourself, others, and your work.

Fear for Your Own Safety

In some cases, traumatic events will leave you scarred and fearing for your own safety all the time. This feeling is natural, and it also gives you an opportunity to strengthen your community. There are a few things you can do to feel more secure in your environment such as paying attention to your surroundings, talk with other people, seek counseling, and speak up if you know someone around you needs help. Sometimes, tragedies might happen on another college campus that makes you feel unsafe on your own campus. As such, seeking counseling or calling the campus police is always a good idea.

Post-trauma at the Workplace

Traumatic events in the workplace will affect your colleagues and coworkers. In such a case, consider having worksite group meetings to discuss individual experience and plan for the future to prevent such incidents from happening again. Because each person experiencestrauma differently, it is best to be patient and understanding. While workplace discussion can help individuals cope with traumatic events, it is still best that everyone get the personalized treatment that they need to overcome.

Traumatized Children

When it comes to traumatic events, children have it the hardest. Such scars continue to stay with them even into adulthood, whether they experienced it first- or second-hand. Common symptoms include fear of going to school, socializing, nightmares, and other regressive behaviors. Thankfully, children are relatively easier to comfort with reassurance, physical touch, and the use of age-appropriate language. Being together with the child might be enough to help them forget about the traumatic events. If left untreated for long, you will need professional help for them when they grow into adults.

Coping with Reactions

Thankfully, there are plenty of ways to cope with stress reactions.

Experience Your Thoughts and Feelings

Sometimes, the best way to overcome is by allowing yourself to experience your thoughts and feelings. Some people deny those feelings because they think that it is unnatural. The reality is you are normal and have normal reactions.

While you are at it, it is also worth talking about your thoughts and feelings. Some of the worst things you can do to yourself is bottling your emotions. Remember that there are always people who are willing to listen to you. Talk to them to get your worries off your chest. Alternatively, you can seek professional health from campus and community resources. Consult a mental health professional if you must. Most of the time, the severity of stress reactions will diminish over time. Seeking professional assistance is recommended if your symptoms persist, causing you discomfort, or that the severity increases over time.

Take Care of Yourself

It is easy to neglect yourself when you are overwhelmed with grief. During those periods, take extra good care of your body by watching what and how much you eat, your alcohol/caffeine/sugar/medicine intake. You might be tempted to use alcohol, drugs, or nicotine to relieve pain, but they only make matters worse. Eat healthily, get enough rest, and take care of yourself as you would someone you care about.

Meanwhile, there is no rush to recovery. Take as much time as you need to recover. Spend time with people you love and care about. Take breaks, plan out some fun things to do, and basically do fun and positive things to forget about the bad memories.

If you have problems concentrating on work or class, you should also talk to your boss or professor about how you should handle your workload while still having enough time to recover.

Have Empathy

When you are handling stressful memories or those who are going through them, it is worth remembering that people experience the same thing differently. So, try to be flexible and understanding. Remember that when people are stressed, they react differently from what you would normally expect.

Moderate Your News Intake

If the trauma is widely publicized, then you should be careful of how the media reports affect you.While information is helpful, you might want to limit yourself. You do not want to know more than you should. If anything, perhaps it is best to hold off learning anything until you are ready to face the truth.

Recognizing Emotions

Everyone has been through one of those moments when the project you have spent weeks on was suddenly canceled, or when your favorite coworker was laid off, or when a customer snapped at you unfairly, or when your boss gives you more work even when you are already overloaded, and then blame you when you cannot do everything. Frustrating, is it not?

In your personal life, the first thing you might do is scream from the top of your lungs, because you know that you did not sign up for any of this. Or, if you are the quieter type, you might just go hide in a corner and feel bad for yourself momentarily, both of these are not healthy. In your professional life, such behaviors are intolerable and could cost you your entire career.

Stressful situations are very common in the workplace, especially the one that is facing budget cuts, staff layoffs, and department changes. It will be more and more difficult for you to manage your emotions under such circumstances. Unfortunately, you are expected to do so. After all, when the next layoff happens, the management will choose who can keep their head under pressure, and that might not be you if you snapped. No matter how stressful the situation really is, you are the one responsible for your reaction because it is a choice.

So, why only negative emotions, you might ask? What about positive emotions? Well, many people do not need to know how to manage their positive emotions because they do not affect others negatively. As long as you share positive emotions constructively and professionally, everyone will benefit from it immensely.

Common Negative Emotions in the Workplace

Professor of management Cynthia Fisher from Bond University conducted a study in 1997 called "Emotions at Work: What Do People Feel, and How Should We Measure It?" According to the research, the most common negative emotions workers feel at work include frustration, irritation, worry, nervousness, anger, aggravation, dislike, disappointment, and unhappiness in the workplace.

Frustration or Irritation

You usually feel frustrated when you feel stuck, trapped, or unable to move on in some way. Examples include a colleague blocking your favorite project, a disorganized boss that cannot maintain their punctuality, or simply being put on hold for too long. Whatever it is, it is important to deal with such emotion as soon as possible because frustration or irritation can lead to more negative emotions such as anger. There are a few ways to deal with frustration.

First, stop and assess the situation. This is one of the best things you can do for yourself. Mentally stop yourself and look at the situation. Ask yourself why you feel frustrated or irritated and write it down. Make sure your description is specific. For example, if you are irritated at your boss because they always show up late for your meeting, at least you have more time to prepare yourself in advance, or that you have more time to relax a bit. This leads us to the second solution.

Think about the positive of the situation. This forces you to look at situations in a different way. This small change in your thinking can help improve your mood. It is also worth mentioning that most people do not want to deliberately annoy you. If they do something that annoys you, remember that it is not personal. There is no need to get mad. Just move on.

You might also want to think back to the last time you feel frustrated. The situation most likely worked out just fine for you after a short while, right? Then, your frustration or irritation might not have done much to help the situation, either. So, they will not help you now, either.

Worry or Nervousness

Many people often feel worried or nervous when there is a large number of layoffs, as the number keeps increasing nowadays. You might now know when you will be next, even things are looking fine right now. This worry can get out of control very easily if you allow it. This can be very damaging to your mental health, productivity, and willingness to take risks. Here are a few suggestions to deal with worrying.

First, do not surround yourself with worry and anxiety. For instance, if your coworkers gather in the break room to talk about job cuts, stay away from there. While they have the right to be worried about their own job security, you should not concern yourself with something that you cannot really control. Worrying would only lead to more worrying, which is not healthy for anyone.

A good way to calm yourself down is, again, breathing. Slow your breathing and your heart rate down. Take in a deep breath and exhale slowly. Focus on your breathing and nothing else. Repeat for at least five times.

Instead of worrying about the situation, think of how to improve it. After all, worrying will not change anything, if not make things worse. If you find yourself worrying all the time, write down all of your worries in a notebook, and schedule a time to address them individually. Until then, you should be able to stop worrying because you already set a time in the future to deal with them. When the time comes, you can conduct a proper risk analysis around those problems and take the necessary actions to mitigate any risks.

Anger or Aggravation

Anger is perhaps one of the most destructive emotion that you can experience in the workplace, and it is the only emotion that many of us do not handle very well. If you have problems managing your anger at work, then learning to control it is the first thing you should do to keep your job. There are a few ways to do this.

First and foremost, look out for any early signs of anger. Only you know the signs of anger when it is cooking up inside you, so learn to identify them when they start. Preventing your anger from starting is the best course of action. Here, you should always remember that you are the one who chooses to react in any situation. While our instinct tells us to throw a fit, it does not mean that it is the best course of action.

Again, stopping yourself is the best way to deal with any kinds of emotions. When you start to get angry, drop whatever you are doing, close your eyes and take deep breaths as mentioned above. This cools you down and puts you on a more positive frame of mind. Another trick employed by some managers or customer service is offering the angry people some water before starting any discussion. This allows the recipient to practice deep breathing exercise and cool down with the water. The basic idea is that you must interrupt yourself before your anger breaks loose. Stop, take deep breaths, and have some water. By the time you are through, you should be able to think much clearer.

Using the power of imagination also helps. When you are about to start swinging, think of how you look. Because we are conscious of how others perceive us, you can use this initially negative cognitive function to your advantage. For instance, if you are about to shout at your colleague, think of how you would look to others. Your face might be tomato red, you might wave your arms around like a tube man (or skydancer, look it up), which would make you look very unprofessional and silly. Would you want others to see you like this? Would you want to work with someone like that? Most likely not. So, if you think about how you would look and behave when you are angry, it might be discouraging enough to stop you.

Dislike

Working with someone we don't like is inevitable, but it is critical to remain professional, no matter what. Here are some suggestions to deal with people you dislike.

First, always be respectful. If you have to work with someone you don't really get along, then set aside your pride and ego. Treat others as you would want others to treat yourself. This is the golden rule. Just because they behave unprofessionally does not give you the right to do the same. If anything, treating others with respect and courtesy even when they do not do the same towards you makes you look even better in the workplace.

At the same time, be assertive. If the other person is being rude and unprofessional, call them out and explain that you refuse to be treated that way. If they do not return the favor of treating you properly, walk away. Be the one to set examples.

Disappointment or Unhappiness

Dealing with these two emotions can be difficult at work and they are the most detrimental to your productivity. If you have just suffered a big disappointment, your energy and productivity will be low. You might be afraid of taking risks, and these will hold you back from achieving. There are a few ways to deal with this problem.

First, examine your mindset. It is important to remember that things will not always go your way, and that is fine. If things will always go as planned, then life would not be a road full of hills and valley. It would be a straight road, which makes thing a lot less exciting.

It is also worth adjusting your goal because you probably went wrong somewhere in the goal-setting process. If you find that you did not reach a goal, that does not mean that you should just give it up. Examine it again and make a small change, such as delaying the deadline.

Writing down your thoughts is the best way to cope with emotions, and coping with disappointment or unhappiness is no exception. Jot down exactly what is bothering you. Is it your co-worker? Is it your career path? Is it because you are underperforming and overloaded? Identify the problem, then think of ways to deal with it. After all, you are the one who has the power to change your situation.

Finally, smile. It sounds strange, silly even, to force yourself a smile. But even if you only manage to get a grimace, you can feel better instantly. This is just the way our brain is wired. Alternatively, try laughing. Laughing at how ridiculous your situation is can cheer your up.

Improving Emotional Intelligence

This section covers techniques on how to improve EI that does not fit quite well in other contexts, especially in leadership which we will talk about later.

EI in Relationship

Marriage is a very serious commitment, and many people struggle to maintain a healthy one. Some people wonder if being emotionally intelligent in a relationship means giving in to your partner's influence and, if so, how to do it.

There is a Japanese martial art called Aikido, a central principle of which called yield to win uses a method of using your opponent's momentum against them to win a right, rather than brute forcing them into submission. That way, you can conserve energy and choose much more efficient and effective tactics. What we can learn here is that yielding to win means accepting, understanding, and allowing your partner's feelings, needs, and perspective into your decision-making process. Basically, you just listen to your partner, making compromises until you both are satisfied. This is giving ground to find a win-win solution. When both sides learn how to accept their partner's influence, the outcome is often very wonderful and healthy for the relationship.

While marriage can last through moments of anger, criticisms, complaints, or even an extended period of negativity if the conflict is managed in a healthy and respectful way. That is why conflict is good for couples, as it opens up opportunities for them to grow as a couple. However, things will take a turn for the worst if they match negativity with negativity instead of making amends to de-escalate the conflict. Mahatma Gandhi once said, "An eye for an eye will make the world blind."

This shows that snapping back during an argument is the worst thing you can do. It does not solve the problem nor help form a compromise. Shutting out your partner is not the way to go as it takes two to make a marriage work. So, all couples have to honor and respect each other. So, how do you accept your partner's influence?

Micro-Moments

You might have heard of the phrase "It's the little things," or some variants of that. This is the one thing you need to always keep in mind. Culture had blown the image of romance out of proportion, especially of the things that make passion sizzle in a marriage. You might already have an idea that expensive jewelry or a romantic getaway is the key to a woman's heart, or that sexy dresses are the key to that of a man's. What really matters though is the dull moments of relationships that are the most significant of them all.

Think of the time when you two had dinner together and talk about life rather than binge watch Netflix in silence, or when you used to touch each other tenderly as you pass each other in the house. You might have experienced those things and taken those small moments for granted. In reality, many people would kill just to relive those moments. This comes as no big surprise as love is cultivated during the tough grind of everyday life. These little moments might seem meaningless, but they offer a level of connection that is the most meaningful of them all.

During those little moments, your partner may try to bid for your attention in many seemingly insignificant ways. For example, when you two are out grocery shopping, and your partner asked whether you have milk at home, saying "I can't remember, let's grab some just to be safe" is very different than just shrugging your shoulders apathetically.

The main reason couples fight is not about money or in-laws, or sex. It is actually the fact that they are unable to connect emotionally. So, make an effort to connect emotionally during those little moments of love.

The Love Piggy Bank

Think of it this way. Every time you remain connected emotionally in love with your special someone, you put a unit of it into a piggy bank and use it during hard times. If you fight often and remain emotionally disconnected, you will also deposit a negative unit. During hard times, if your positive saving is more than the negative one, then you two are less likely to distrust each other during those moments. If not, then trust and intimacy will erode away bit by bit. There are a few ways to reconnect with your partner.

Responds to Bids for Affection

As mentioned earlier, your partner will make bids for your attention/affection throughout the day. Most of the time, couples ignore each other's emotional needs out of mindlessness, not malice. So, the first step then is to recognize the importance of those little moments. This is important for your marriage, romance, and intimacy. This can be accomplished easily by acting like it was the first day of your marriage/getting together. Those moments must have felt magical for you.

The change form not talking everyday interaction for granted helps a lot in marriage. Helping out around the house is much better than a two-week vacation in a tropical location. Sometimes, we just miss those bids because our partners express it negatively. For example, if the wife said to her husband, "It never occurs to you to empty the dishwasher, does it?" Then the husband might not hear what she was actually trying to say ("Please unload the dishwasher"), he hears criticism, which caused him to react defensively.

If the husband instead says something like, "Oh, you're right. Sorry," and empty the dishwasher, he would score one for himself and might earn a sheepish smile from his wife when she realized that her tone was unnecessary. So, before you start replying defensively, pause for a second and analyze their words. What they say might hide a bid for your affection, and you should respond to it.

Understanding Love Maps

Sometimes, couples assume that their partner feels heard and known. The secret to understanding your partner is not about reading their mind, but rather through the hard work of putting your partner in a position where they can share their thoughts and feelings openly and honestly.

Do you know what your partner is worrying or stressing about at the moment? What are their goals this year? What are their hopes and aspirations? Are they different from last year? Here, you need to do three things to understand each other.

Ask questions, remember the answers, and keep asking questions.

This is the best way to get to know your partner better. Plus, sharing your thoughts and feelings is a lifelong process, hence the third step. After all, what you want to eat can change every day, so does your thoughts and feelings. It is also worth pointing out that the better the questions you ask, the larger the emotional investment both of you make.

Mutual Appreciation and Respect

Everyone has their own personality flaws. Sometimes, your loved one might interrupt you when you are telling a story and tell their side, or when they tell you in an annoyed tone that they just want to sleep when you just want to cuddle. Do you think that these things build affection and respect in a relationship? Of course not.

If you ever catch yourself in a dysfunctional relationship and that you want to try to make your partner "perfect", you might be aware of the fact that it is impossible. Here's the thing. Everyone has their own flaws. You cannot change another person. That is why you should learn to accept the flaws instead because that makes them so special and lovable.

It is also worth remembering that whoever you choose to love, it is implied that you also love the problems that those people have. The reality is that there are no problem-free candidates. A relationship, no matter how perfect it may seem, will have all sort of problems.

When we learned how to accept and love our partners for who they are, it is a lot easier to start making an emotional connection. Whenever you can express your appreciation of something that your partner did right. For instance, say "Thanks for doing that. I noticed you unloaded the dishwasher and I really appreciate it," when you catch your partner doing just that. Whenever you do that, your partner will feel the emotional connection.

Remember, love is not built on an exotic vacation or expensive items. Most of the time, it is the little things in the everyday grind of life that makes love worthwhile.

The 7 Principles

Different kinds of relationships require different things to survive. However, you can never go wrong by following these seven principles.

First, accept your partner "as is". We can never stress this enough. You should never try to change them. You can either like them for what they are or don't. Everyone has their own flaws. You can always live with those flaws, most of the time. The best kind of relationship is when each partner is happy with themselves. If you focus on trying to change your partner, blame kicks in, which is harmful in any relationship.

In addition to accepting your partner as they are, take the time and tell them that you appreciate what they did for you and the relationship as a whole. Point out all the small things you like about your partner and be open and sincere about it. Appreciation is the true language of love, and you would often notice that people always describe their partner as if they are some superhero. This is an exaggeration, of course, but this is also a manifestation of love, respect, and affection.

Agree to disagree. Suppose that you and your partner have different plans to enjoy the weekend. You can insist that your partner should come along with you because they made a promise about it at some point in the past, or because you should be together when everyone else come with their partner to that particular place. Alternatively, you can also listen to your partner and understand their need to follow their plan, understand their point of view and connect with them. Show that you understand them and then explain your own point of view. Be open and honest about your needs and wants. Then, whatever happens next is really not important. What really matters is that you handle the problem the best way possible because you just built trust, confidence, attachment, and well-being with your partner.

Even if you have disagreements, you should always support your partner, no matter what. Helping your partner achieve their goal is a very important thing for your relationship. Even when things go awry for your partner, and what you have disagreed, supporting your partner helps prevent the relationship from being damaged.If things go well, celebrate and be honestly happy for your partner.If you feel that whatever your partner is pursuing the wrong goal, you can argue and reason, but you should always be their fan. When your partner realizes that whatever they are doing is wrong, understand that this is a right they have. After all, we are humans and errors are inevitable. The last thing your partner wants to hear is "I told you so". Alternatively, they need connection, love, and support. This is what will keep the relationship together.

Accepting the fact that your friend or partner should not necessarily do what you want them to do can be difficult to grasp. After all, they might know something that you don't, not to mention that they are not your child nor your puppy. Instead, try changing these demands into preferences. You should not say that your friends should come to the party with you, but show them that you would appreciate it if they do. Most of the time, transforming demands into preferences gives your partner or friends options and actually has a higher chance of convincing them to join you in whatever you plan to do.

Body Language

Body language is an important component in communication that people use to reveal their true feelings and emotions. Our facial expression, posture, and gesture say a lot more about us than what we voice out.

When we can read body language, we can use it to our advantage. We can understand what someone is actually trying to say and understand how people really respond to your what you say and do. We can also take a step back and observe our body language and adjust it accordingly to make us appear more positive, engaging, and approachable.

Reading Body Language

More specifically, the negative one. Being aware of it in others can help us pick up on unspoken problems or bad feelings. There are a few nonverbal signs you need to look out for.

Defensiveness and Difficult Conversations

It is a fact of life at work to deal with difficult or tense conversations. Maybe you work in customer support or retail and have to deal with a difficult customer, or you work as a supervisor and need to talk to someone about their poor performance. In an ideal situation, these problems would be resolved calmly, but this is wishful thinking at best. They often are complicated by feelings of nervousness, defensiveness, stress, or even anger. Try as we might hide them, these emotions are often evident in our body language.

If someone is feeling disengaged, disinterested, or unhappy, they might cross their arms in front of their body, putting up minimal or tense facial expression, keeping their body turned away from you, and having their eyes downcast and maintaining little eye contact.

Though these clues, you can adjust what you say and how you say it so you can bring them back into the conversation by making them feel more at ease and receptive to your message.

Avoiding Unengaged Audiences

When you want to deliver a presentation or to work in a group, you need everyone to be engaged. There are a few signs that people might be disinterested or bored with what you are saying.

They might be sitting slumped with heads downcast, gazing at something else or staring blankly into space, fidgeting, picking at clothes, or fiddling with objects, or writing or doodling.

If they display any of these signs, you can do something about it. The best way to bring them back into the conversation is by asking them direct questions or inviting them to contribute their ideas.

Projecting Positive Body Language

You can add strength to the verbal message or ideas that you want to put out there when you use positive body language, in addition to preventing you from sending mixed or confused signals. Here, we will look at some basic postures you can adopt in order to project confidence and openness.

Confident First Impression

Making the right first impression is critical. There are a few ways to achieve this.

First, adopt an open posture. Remain relaxed but do not slouch. Stand or stand upright and put your hands by your sides. Try not to stand with your hands on your hips because this makes you look larger, which can communicate aggression or a desire to dominate.

A firm handshake is a strong projector of confidence, but do not get carried away. The worst thing you can do to your handshake is by making it awkward or painful for the other person. If it does, then the other person might see you as rude or aggressive.

Maintaining good eye contact is just as crucial. Try to hold the other person's gaze for a few seconds at a time, but avoid turning it into a starting match. Good eye contact will show that you are interested and listening.

Finally, avoid touching your face. There is a common perception that people who are not telling the truth often touch their face when answering questions, but that is not always the case. Still, avoid fiddling with your hair or touching your mouth or nose if you want to come across as trustworthy.

Public Speaking

Projecting positive body language is also crucial in public speaking as it helps you engage people, to project confidence, or to mask presentation nerves. Here are a few tips.

Start by having a positive posture. Stand or sit upright, your shoulders back, and your arms at your sides or in front of you. Avoid slouching or putting your hands in your pockets because these make you look disinterested.

Also, keep your head up. It should be upright and level. Leaning too far forward or backward can make you look aggressive or arrogant.

In any presentation, you would practice beforehand, so why not practice your body language as well? Try to relax while standing with your weight distributed evenly. Keep one foot slightly in front of the other so you can maintain your posture.

Finally, use open hand gestures. Spread your hands apart with your palms facing slightly toward your audience in front of you. Make sure that the palms of your hands are visible. This is a subtle sign that indicates a willingness to communicate and share ideas. The reason why Mark Zuckerberg was perceived as not trustworthy during the Congressional hearing is the fact that he smiled awkwardly (always squint when you smile) and that he never shows his palms when he spoke. Also, keep your upper arms close to your body, avoid overexpression because people might pay more attention to your hands than to what you are saying.

Also, if you notice that your audience's concentration is starting to slip, try leaning slightly forward while you speak. This might help you regain their attention because this suggests that you are taking them into your confidence. Alternatively, use the power of silence. Many of us are so used to listening that silence is almost as shocking as someone yelling. Speak and pause for a few seconds and see if people start paying attention again.

Interviews, Reflection, and Negotiations

Body language can help you remain calm in situations where negative emotions can run high, such as during a negotiation or a performance review. Here are a few tips to reduce tension and demonstrate openness:

First, try mirroring. Basically, it is copying the body language of the person you are talking to. That does not mean that you have to copy every single gesture that the other person makes because this makes them uncomfortable, or tells them that you do not take them seriously. Instead, subtly mirror their body language instead to make them feel more at ease and can build rapport.

Again, relax your body. It is quite difficult to keep your emotions at bay, especially during an interview or appraisal. Still, you can make yourself look calm (although you are screaming inside your head) by keeping your hands still, avoid fidgeting with your hair or touching your face.

Finally, look interested. While touching your face or mouth can be seen as a sign of dishonesty, it can also mean that you are thinking. If someone asked you a complex question, it is fine to touch your cheek or stroke your chin briefly, which indicates that you are reflecting your answer carefully before you respond.

Active Listening

In addition to reading body language, you should also learn how to listen actively. With all the listening we have subjected ourselves you, you might think that we would already be good at it. In reality, we are not, and research suggests that we hardly remember more than half of what we hear. To put that into context, half of what you said will go straight over your colleague's', boss', friends', or spouse's head, unless they are great listeners.

Therefore, listening is a skill that we all can benefit from. By becoming a better listener, you can improve your productivity and your ability to influence persuade, and negotiate. Moreover, you can avoid conflict and misunderstanding just by listening better. All of these are important for workplace success. So, how do you become an active listener?

Pay Attention

There is nothing better than giving the speaker undivided attention and acknowledge the message they are delivering. Also, observe their body language because that is just as important as the verbal message. So, look at the speaker directly, put aside distracting thoughts, do not mentally prepare a rebuttal, and avoid distraction.

Show That You Are Listening

This is pretty straightforward because all you need to do is use your body language and gestures to show that you are engaged. Nod occasionally, smile and react genuinely to what they say, make sure your posture is open to show your interest, and encourage the speaker to continue talking by saying "Interesting," "go on", "Uh huh", etc.

Provide Feedback

Sometimes, we understand messages incorrectly because of our personal filters, assumptions, judgments, and beliefs. As a listener, you need to understand what is being said and this might require you to reflect on what is said and ask questions. The best way to do this is paraphrasing. Put what they said into your own words and confirm with the speaker if you understand it correctly. If not, ask questions to clarify certain points. Also, summarize the speaker's comments now and again to ensure that you two are on the same page.

Defer Judgment

Interrupting is rude and a waste of time as it frustrates the speaker and limits full understanding of the message. So, allow the speaker to finish each point before asking questions. Sometimes, the speaker will pause after each point and ask whether you are following. Also, never interrupt with counter-arguments.

Respond Appropriately

Active listening encourages respect and understanding. When you listen, you get more information, perspective, and insights. Attacking the speaker or putting them down does not help anyone. That does not mean that you should just sit there, smile, and nod either.

Be candid, honest, and open in your response and assert your opinions respectfully. Remember that your opinions might just be as wrong to them as theirs to you. Keep in mind what is important here. You are here to take in ideas and knowledge and the other person is there to share it. While debate can be done after the conversation or when the right opportunity presents itself, always

Mindfulness and Relaxation Techniques

Mindfulness has been a subject of study in clinical, professional sports, military, and corporate settings for over 30 years now. The research found that mindfulness is associated with a significant number of benefits such as increased job performance and reduction in stress and anxiety. Many scholars agree that mindfulness is a state of consciousness consisting of awareness and attention. Mindfulness is comprised of three things:

- Clear focus of attention on the present moment, including experience and events
- Ability to change the level of non-judgmental attention
- Awareness of changing attention between the inner self and the outer world

Simply put, you can experience mindfulness by focusing all of your attention on your thoughts, feelings, and actions as they occur. Mindfulness training will be the key to strengthen your emotional self-awareness, which is the ability to recognize our emotions and how they influence our feelings. Thankfully, there are plenty of mindfulness training exercise materials out there. A high-quality mindfulness training program will last about 8 weeks. But we want to focus on a quick and convenient way to practice mindfulness. There is no better solution than taking the time to meditate. You might already be told to take deep breaths to keep your emotions under control. Meditation is basically deep breathing, but with a few extra steps with greater benefits as it allows you to take a look deep inside yourself and understand yourself better. So, how do you meditate properly?

How to Meditate

The entire process is actually very simple and personal. It should not take too much time to prepare everything. However, if you want to reap lasting benefits of meditation, however, you need to dedicate or find a permanent place where you will spend your time meditating.

Props

Meditation will be a lot easier if you have a few props. There are plenty out there that claim to help you meditate, but there is no need to go overboard. All you need is a seat, a timer, and a place to meditate.

For seating, there are three options. You can sit on a chair or sofa if you are starting out with meditation, have back problems, or find that meditation cushion uncomfortable. It keeps your back straight in sitting position as it is crucial in any meditation. Consider switching to a meditation cushion when you are more familiar and comfortable with meditation.

A meditation cushion is the most common thing that people sit on when they meditate. It is so popular because of the fact that it is the easiest to sit on with an upright position. That, in turns, helps you stay alert and keep the quality of the meditation high. Of course, a meditation cushion does not have a backrest, but when you slump against it, you will lose focus. The meditation cushion forces you to keep your back straight, and maintaining that healthy form as well as keeping you focused on yourself.

If you are tall, have legs problems or that meditation cushion is just too uncomfortable and counterproductive to your meditation, you might want to give the meditation bench a shot. Just like the meditation cushion, you still need to sit upright without the backrest so you will not have the urge to slump. What makes this different from the meditation cushion is that it absorbs more weight than the cushion, so it takes off the pressure from your legs, and make meditation comfortable for you.

The timer is another crucial tool to help you meditate. When you close your eyes and go on a journey of self-discovery that is meditation, it is easy to lose track of time. Having a timer does come in handy, and it is built into most phones. There is really no need for you to buy a physical meditation timer when your phone works just as well. All that you really need from the timer is to tell you when you should stop meditating so you don't have to break away from the trance just to look at the time.

Location is also crucial for your meditation. You need to find a place with enough light (but not too much), open enough to let the fresh air comes through, and with enough space, for you to be able to open up. It is worth mentioning that the place should help you feel relaxed even before you begin, so the decoration or the color of the room should also reflect that. One more thing to consider is the noise. It should be kept at a minimum level so you will not get distracted.

How to Sit

If you have watched any clips related to meditation, you will see that there are many forms of meditation. Do not fret. While there is little information given and that beginners often are left wondering if they are even sitting correctly, it all boils down to personal preference, which is exactly why there are so many forms in the first place. However, they share some common traits.

Close the eyes fully or keep them partially open. If you can focus on your breathing with your eyes closed, do that. If you feel sleepy with your eyes closed, open your eyes a bit and focus on the nearest object in your sight. Experiment and see what works for you.

For your head, tilt it slightly upward so to open up your body and helps it relax. Plus, it takes pressure off your neck when you lean your head back a bit, not to mention that it helps with your bad neck posture (slumping forward).

For the hands and legs, put them wherever you feel the most comfortable. You can intertwine your fingers, put one palm over other, or just put them on your laps or knees. You can cross your legs, put them in a pretzel-like position, or just put them normally when you sit on a chair.

While there are several types of meditations out there, you should always meditate in a way that allows you to be comfortable while remaining alert. Comfort and alertness should be your top priority. If you are uncomfortable, it will be hard to concentrate. If you are too comfortable, you might fall asleep. Find that perfect balance that allows you to be comfortable but alert at the same time. In the end, the pose, form, or placements of hands and legs are up to you. You choose which one is the best for you, and stick to it.

Meditating

The one thing that you need to control (and might be the most difficult thing to control) is your attention. In your life, your attention may be scattered to many things at once. Your phone, the conversation, the time, the work, and many other things. Meditation challenges you to gather all of your focus and put it all in a single place: your breathing.

Sounds easy enough, right? Probably. Now that you have everything ready, you can start meditating on the following steps.

Get Comfortable: Go to your meditation place, get the timer ready, and don't forget your chair or meditation cushion or meditation bench. It might help you focus if you dim the lights a bit, or just shut them all off so you can focus better.

Set Your Timer: If you are just starting out, then you should go for 5 minutes of meditation. Some go for 10 minutes or even 30 minutes. We recommend you to start small first. If you are unfamiliar with meditation, you will find that keeping your attention on your breathing for 5 minutes can be difficult.

Focus: Start the timer, and close your eyes and your mouth. Focus on your breathing as it comes in and out. Here, you can focus on any aspects of your breathing. Whatever works best for you, of course. Some focus on how the air enters and exit the nose. Some focus on how it inflates and deflates the lungs. Some focus on the stomach. You can even focus on the sound you make when you breathe. Pacing is also important. Keep it slow and steady. Take slow, and deep breaths. Observe the way you breathe, but try your very best to keep your mind empty. This leads to our third step.

Keep Your Mind Empty: Try your best to not think of anything. Focus all of your attention and mind on the breath that you are taking. It is easy to get distracted. Do not worry about how well you do your meditation. Just focus on doing it. If you do get distracted and your mind wanders, do your best to gently guide it back to your breaths. It can be just as easy to become frustrated when your mind wanders constantly, especially if you are just starting out. You tend to lose focus when you exhale because that is subtler than when you inhale and it can be hard to concentrate on. If you find it hard to concentrate, try counting your breath when you exhale. That way, you can concentrate on your breath when you breathe in, and concentrate on the number when you breathe out. We recommend you count up to 5 and then reset to 0.

Additional Tips

There are a few more things you need to keep in mind when you meditate so you can reap all the benefits of meditation.

- **Try to do it first thing in the morning, and before bed:** Not only that you will not forget to do it on a daily basis, meditation also serves as the transition from a relaxed state of the body after a restful sleep to the more active state when you get on with your daily life. You can skip the step entirely and launch yourself into the day full of stressful events, but your body may not catch on and you will feel tired. It will also be hard for you to focus when you work. Meditation is a great bedtime routine as well.

- **Develop a loving attitude:** When you meditate, many things (good and bad) will come up in your mind. Look at them as if they are there to help you. A way to develop positive thinking is by seeing everything in a kind, and loving way.

- **Don't worry too much about how you're doing it:** Some people become frustrated or worried that they did not meditate properly when they get distracted for a few seconds during their session. The thing is, there is no way you could meditate perfectly. There will be flaws and you will get distracted sometimes. When your mind wanders, gently guide it back to your breathing. You will get better at this as time passes.

- **Don't ignore whatever that comes:** Meditation is also a journey of self-discovery. When you meditate, most of the small and insignificant things will vanish. However, some deeper, pressing issues tend to arise. Those issues are most likely the source of your anger, anxiety, or frustration. You will recognize them as they come. Although you should just brush it aside when you meditate, it is worth staying with them for a moment. It can be tricky to stay with those thoughts without feeling the negativity, but it can help you pinpoint the source of your sorrow so you can address them later.

- **Befriend yourself and your emotions:** As mentioned earlier, meditation is more than just to relax. It is also a journey of self-discovery. When you meditate, be aware of your own thoughts. Chances are they are responsible for your behavior. However, observe yourself in a friendly way, and do not criticize yourself too badly. Give yourself some love and try to understand yourself.

- **Commit:** This is where most beginners fail. They tried it once or twice, and then give up and say that meditation does not help them at all. In reality, it does. All it takes is some efforts.

Develop a habit of meditation on a daily basis, and you will soon notice the difference.

- **Comfort and alertness:** We talked about this before, but this needs to be stressed again. No matter what type or form of meditation you practice, comfort and alertness should always be a high priority. If you are uncomfortable, it will be hard for you to concentrate. If you are too comfortable, you run the risk of snoozing off. Find that perfect balance which you can be comfortable but alert at the same time. In the end, the pose, form, or placements of hands and legs are up to you. You choose which one is the best for you, and stick to it.

- **Focus:** If you find it hard to focus on your breathing, or want to try something a little bit more difficult and different, then there are other alternatives that you could try out. You could try to focus on a certain part of the body at a time. Be aware of how that body part feels. You can even try to work your way up from your feet up to your head during meditation. Alternatively, you can place your attention on the light in the room. You can even switch up your point of focus on a daily basis. One day, you focus on the sounds, and the next day, you can focus on the light.

- **When you're done, smile:** Meditation is also the process of giving yourself the attention you need and deserve. In order to develop positive thinking, smile after you have finished your meditation. Be thankful for yourself that you allow yourself some quality time to meditate. Give yourself a pat on the shoulder as if to say "Nice job" for sticking to your commitment. Everyone needs some self-love, and there is not much else to do to feed yourself just that.

Common Mistakes

There are many ways to meditate, that much is true. Some aspects of meditation can be modified to fit your own preferences, although many people pay a little too much attention to detail. The most common mistakes people make when they are meditating is the way that they think.

- **Judging the Experience:** When you meditate, the goal is to keep you breathing steadily and your head clear. It is meant to give your head a break, the silence that it deserves. However, it is also the practice of patience and gratitude. We mentioned before how important it is to keep your mind and heart at peace when you meditate. Beginners tend to worry whether they are doing it right, or that the meditation that they are practicing is a good one. Instead, stop worrying and focus on the fact that you are practicing meditation. Focus on yourself and the stillness of emotions.

- **Props:** There are many of them that can help you focus. However, it is also worth mentioning that you do not need them to meditate. In fact, they might even distract you from the meditation. Meditation is all about inner peace, and you do not need external objects to achieve that. That does not mean that props are worthless. Try to keep them to a minimum. Keep the ones that actually keep you awake or focused.

- **Over-complications:** Nowadays, you can find hundreds of meditation techniques that have modern twists on ancient practices. While science has contributed to these modern meditation techniques, it is worth noting that they may lack the spiritual experience. Traditional meditation techniques have been developed and have thousands of years of experience in spiritual growth, and that is what makes them a better choice for serious practitioners. Modern meditation techniques can be fun to try out, but you should stick to the traditional ones.

- **Guided Meditations:** This is a type of meditation which we will discuss later. Basically, it helps beginners and experts alike unlock the key to inner peace easier. However, it is not recommended that you use it every time when you meditate. While helpful in itself, you should learn how to access that place of silence and peace on your own. Otherwise, your own journey is not worthwhile. Of course, that does not mean that you should ditch this meditation altogether. You just need to maintain a healthy balance between the guided meditations and solo meditations.

- **Spice things up:** Meditation can get repetitive and boring very quickly. When it does, you will find it hard to keep meditating. How do you avoid that? Simple. You can mix things up a bit to keep it interesting. Try meditating with your eyes open, or with soothing ambient music (if you haven't already). If you are feeling adventurous, then you can even try meditating while you are working. All you need to do is to keep your head clear and breathing deep and constant. You do not really need to sit down in a meditating position in order to start meditating. Just make sure that you are comfortable with the environment before you start.

Progressive Muscular Relaxation

Progressive muscle relaxation is a deep meditation that operates under the assumption that the muscles tense up in response to stressful thoughts. By relaxing the muscles, it is possible to release the built-up stress inside as well. It is also an effective way to relieve insomnia and reduce symptoms of certain types of chronic pain.

This relaxation technique works to counter the infamous fight-or-flight reaction that causes a lot of stress. This response is a common reaction to fear or danger, which is hardly the case in reality. Nowadays, some harmless situations can trigger this response and it triggers physical symptoms such as accelerated heart rate, sweating, shaking, and shortness of breath thanks to the stress hormones. Since muscle pain, stiffness, and tension are common symptoms of stress and anxiety, this relaxation relieves stress by addressing those symptoms. It forces a relaxation response, calming the mind and lowering the heart rate by practicing slow, deep breathing and muscle relaxation routines.

This technique was described by Edmund Jacobson in about 1930. It is based upon his premise that mental calmness is a natural result of physical relaxation. Progressive muscle relaxation is very easy to learn and it only requires from 10 to 20 minutes a day to practice. While these techniques are effective against a wide number of conditions, some of which cannot be treated by medicine, it is worth noting that it can take a lot of therapy session to complete.

Progressive muscle relaxation is useful for treating conditions that medicine fails to cure, such as dementia. Even if the condition can be treated, some people prefer practicing these techniques than taking medicine because there is little or no risk associated with them. These techniques serve as a useful supplementary treatment for some psychological conditions as well. It is shown to be effective against withdrawal symptoms such as craving.

PMR: Step by Step

Start by finding a quiet place free from distractions. Lay down on the floor or recline in a chair. Loosen any tight clothing and remove glasses or contacts. Put the hands on the laps or on the arms rest. Then, take in a few deep breaths slowly. It is recommended to do a diaphragmatic breathing exercise throughout the entire exercise by synchronizing the breaths with the tension and the relaxation of the muscle in each area, but do not hold the breath. Some people find it more comfortable to work from the top of their head down to their toes. Others prefer doing it in the opposite direction. While this guide follows the former direction, it is still applicable to the latter method. Just like meditation, it is important to focus on each area of the muscle as it tightens and relaxes. It is okay if the mind wanders. Just guide it back to the muscle and proceed normally. Another thing worth noting is that one should not tighten the muscles to strain it.

Starting with the forehead muscle by raising the brows as high as possible, hold for about 5 seconds and then quickly release that tension. Give it a 5 to 10 seconds break and then move on to the cheek muscle. Smile as widely as possible. The mouth and cheeks should feel tense. Hold for 5 seconds and release quickly again. Do the same with the head by gently pulling it back to look at the ceiling, hold, release, and pause.

Moving down to the hand, clench the right fist, hold, release, and pause. Do the same to the right forearm, the upper arm, and then the entire arm. Make sure that the muscle in each area is tightened and feel the tension and relaxation. Do the same for the shoulders by lifting them as high up as possible. Repeat the process for the left hand, and then do the shoulders again.

Then, tense the upper back by pulling the shoulders back, hold, release, and pause. Work on the lower back by arching it. Then, do the same for the buttocks. After that, work on the legs by first tensing the entire right leg and thigh. Pull the toes inside and feel the tension in the calves. Repeat for the left leg.

Finally, bring the entire relaxation session to a close by feeling a wave of relaxation going from the head to toe. Relax and breathe slow and deep breaths for a few minutes.

Emotional Intelligence and Leadership

Leadership skills are fairly recognizable in many contexts such as the workplace, classroom, politics, volunteer organization, and even family. Good leaders are expected to be able to strategize, plan, have a vision, and take the initiative to accomplish their goals. These skills are most often seen when working in a team setting.

However, leadership skills are not limited to those stated above. There are many things that a good leader possess. You may be highly trained and are proficient in your field, but your skills that contribute to your ability to work in unison with others smoothly and lead them to success may be lacking.

This is where emotional intelligence comes in. Because emotional intelligence governs knowing your own emotions and that of others and taking action based on that knowledge to cultivate a productive relationship, one can never overstress how critical EI is in leadership. It is not hard to see the value of emotional intelligence for leaders. Think about a great boss you have worked with in the past. You must have felt very comfortable asking him questions, raising your concerns, and requesting him to meet certain needs at the workplace. They would most likely listen to you and make sure you feel supported. Even when you two had disagreements, it will be a healthy, productive debate that would likely end up in a compromise. Maybe you have grown so close to such a boss that you have immense respect for them, and they return that same amount of respect to you, to the point that you see them as a close friend. You no longer see them as a superior who breaths down your neck whenever you work. You would feel like they are the one who asked you a favor to help them in the company and pays you for it instead of working for them and get paid.

This kind of connection between employee and manager is the kind of relationship you should have with your lover. This involves keeping a positive perspective, validating each other's positions despite the disagreement, and basically being respectful even when the argument becomes heated. It is a healthy way to maintain a relationship and both sides would feel supported and valued.

In the workplace, as you are very familiar with, teamwork is critical when you need to achieve a goal, especially a difficult, long-term one. Even lofty goals can cause intense emotions such as anger, worry, or disappointment if things are not going well. When things do go well, everyone would feel excited and they do everything with enthusiasm. They wait in anticipation for their work to bear fruit and celebrate together. A good example of such a display of emotions can be found in cohesive sports teams. They celebrate together, roll around the grass when things go well for them. When things go awry, they lift each other up. Even a game based solely on physical prowess and teamwork requires emotional strength if the team wants to succeed.

Still, all of these emotions can still lead to immense stress, even the good one, under the challenging circumstances at work. As such, understanding and managing your emotions and that of others in a team setting is one of the key skills a good leader should have.

Good Leadership

EI is the difference between a tyrannical boss and a leader that everyone is willing to sacrifice their personal time and expense just to see a project fly. Everyone has envisioned their dream job to be something that they enjoy doing. In reality, we do not really enjoy doing anything. Our dream job is more about the environment than the work itself. If we feel a great sense of belonging at work, we would likely not leave that job no matter how little it pays us. The responsibility of cultivating this environment falls upon the leader. As such, it is absolutely necessary for a leader to have a high degree of EI. No matter what leaders set out to do, their success depends on how they do it, not what they do. It does not matter if it is creating a strategy or getting the team to act, nothing will fly if the leader cannot drive their subordinates' emotions in the right direction, even if they get everything right.

There is no need to look far for examples. Think about your previous jobs when you have worked under a manager with a negative attitude. While their expertise and experience are unquestionable, how they do their job and communicate with their employees are. Think about how you and your coworkers may have felt around that manager. While you might be afraid of losing your job, you were just afraid of him. There was no respect. You only felt undervalued, disrespected, and not motivated at all. In that workplace environment, it is a lot easier to keep your head down, mouth shut, and do just enough to keep your job. When everyone feels that way, they hardly feel happy in whatever it is they do. Productivity will only decrease and work will not go anywhere. Worse, there will be challenging problems down the line when the team is assigned to do something remotely complicated.

It is not just in the workplace either. This also applies to romantic relationships. Resentment, disconnection, separation, or even divorce are some examples of poor outcomes born from a negative outlook. It is hard to change to a positive outlook when negative sentiment overrides kicks in. On the other hand, enthusiasm, respect, appreciation, combined with validation and emotional support can be very contagious, in a good way! Positivity breeds positivity, after all. Emotions play a crucial role in performance and productivity, teams whose member feel emotionally supported and appreciated for their valiant efforts and successes will most likely be happier and even more productive. It is basically a positive feedback loop. When they are happy and productive, they are more likely to be successful, which makes them even happier and even more productive. Who would not want that?

Not only the employers, but the employees want that too.

This applies everywhere where there is a leader. This can be the sous chef in a restaurant kitchen, a foreman on a factory floor, a head nurse in an emergency room, a CEO in the boardroom, or even a high school teacher in a classroom. Effective emotional understanding and management help team member work together and be more productive, effective while making them feel more valued and understood.

Adaptation

When leaders have a high degree of emotional intelligence, they are also able to adapt to changing circumstance. As you may already know, the workplace is anything but predictable. As such, knowing how to adapt to ever-changing circumstances is very crucial. In fact, Chinese president Xi told attendees at a job fair that EI helps individual to be more adaptable in the society. Being aware of, understanding, and managing your emotions and that of others proves to be immensely helpful when you need to navigate through the ever-changing world and become a successful leader.

EI is a key leadership skill, according to the Harvard Business Review. Leaders need to be masterful at managing their relationships in a positive way if they really want to be effective. Being a leader of a group requires you to have a very strong connection with those who work for you. While we have seen our fair share of good leaders in history, they all have one thing in common. They have a high EI level. Of course, we have talked extensively about how EI is the key factor in your success, but that does not mean that IQ and technical skills are irrelevant. They also matter, but they are the basic requirement for any positions. EI is basically the sine qua non of relationship because you need it to be a great leader, even if you have the best training in the world, an incisive, analytical mind, and an endless supply of smart ideas. Again, EI alone will not be enough to get you to the top of the corporate ladder, but you will be more effective and have a better chance of doing so if you have the basic requirements down. Moreover, emotions are always changing so adaptability is key to be a great leader.

Leadership and Performance

The bottom is critical when it comes to the workplace, especially business. Managers and executives are often held responsible for both successes and failures. According to Dr. Jack Zenger and Dr. Joseph Folkman, co-founders of the leadership development and training form known as Zenger Folkman, there are nine key traits that many successful leaders have. They have compiled a report of over 100,000 direct reports from employees about their leaders from hundreds of companies in various fields and studied the pattern in all of them. These are the nine key traits:

Inspiration and Motivation

Leaders who have a high level of energy and enthusiasm are better at motivating and inspiring others. They have a special aura that energizes their team to achieve even the most difficult goals and increase everyone's performance. Unfortunately, many leaders oftenneglect their own team members because they focus too much on accomplishing tasks in their job description.Although employees will do an adequate job even without inspiration (just so not to get fired), they tend to perform with more effort and energy that can be the difference between success and failure if they are inspired. The bottom line is, every leader needs to find ways to inspire their employees to push themselves.

Driving for Results

The drive to achieve results is critical to success. You can see this as an extension of the previous factor because motivation requires both the drive for results and inspiration. The former is the push force and the latter is the pull force, and the lack of each one of them will result in the lack of motivation. As such, a healthy balance is needed between the two. Leaders who can drive for results are good at getting people to remain focused and go for the highest priority goals. They create high standards of excellence for the workgroup and are not afraid to request that their employees perform better while reminding them continually of their progress in relation to the goal.

Strategic Perspective

The previous two mobilize employees so things can happen, but this one controls the direction of those activities. Leaders should provide their team with a sense of direction and purpose so everyone feels more committed and satisfied before, during, and after the work is completed. Such leaders can paint a crystal clear perspective between the bigger picture and the minor details of day-to-day activities. Great leaders are always reinforcing where the organization is heading and highlight the key steps that lead to success. While this might sound a lot like micromanaging, employees really need to be reminded of how their hard work makes a difference and how it helps get the organization closer to success.

Collaboration

This is arguably the most common challenge in today's organizations. There is always some form of lack of cooperation between groups in an organization. What happens is that all groups in an organization are competing for resources and recognition. While you may argue that this boosts performance, it is worth pointing out that an organization needs every single group to do their best so it can perform well. When everyone is competing for resources, they withhold information, leaving customers underserved and stalling work. This lack of synergy and conflict often discourages and frustrates employees. Leaders who can promote a high level of cooperation among the work groups will create a positive and productive atmosphere in the organization. When leaders demonstrate what amazing feats they can achieve with a high level of intergroup cooperation, synergy is created and everyone enjoys the work experience.

Walk the Talk

Honesty and integrity are some of the most basic behavior in creating a satisfied and committed workforce. Leaders need to be the role models upon whom others look up to. As such, they need to set a good example for their workgroup. While there is a saying "Do as I say, and not as I do," no one really wants to come to work on time when the leader is always an hour late. Leaders like that create cynicism and lose trust when they say one thing but do another. Every leaderneeds to look at themselves critically and ask whether they are walking the talk.

Trust

Trust is a very fragile thing. It takes years to build trust, but it can be destroyed in an hour. Leaders can engender trust by being more aware of the concerns, circumstances, and aspirations of others. We trust our friends more than our enemies, after all. Trust is built in different ways, two of which are done through knowledge and expertise because they project confidence in the ability to make informed decisions.

Consistency also reinforces trust because when leaders are consistent and predictable, others are confident and trust the leaders. Moreover, trust can also be built through honesty and integrity. When employees know their employer would never tell them anything that is not accurate and factual, they believe that employer. Consistency is the key to build this kind of trust.

Develops and Supports Others

When leaders work in unison with employees and pus the latter to develop new skills and abilities, they are reinforcing a higher level of employee satisfaction and commitment. Employees who develop new skills perform better and more promotable. Great leaders are happy by the success of others and they can promote greater employee development by creating a learning environment in which people are encouraged to learn from mistakes, take time to analyze their successes, and understand what they got right.

Building Relationships

Leaders who remain connected with issues and concerns of individual workers in the workgroup have employees with more employee satisfaction and commitment. According to the study, these leaders are seen to be able to balance between getting results and caring for the needs of the workers. This does not mean that achieving results is not the focus, though. It is just that those leaders find the sweet spot between individual needs and organizational needs, and demonstrate that they value the individual because those people are the ones who get things done. As such, they create strong positive relationships with team members.

Courage

Leaders with the highest levels of employee satisfaction and commitment are also courageous. They do not back away from conflicts. They deal with problems head-on. When they see the first signs of problems in their teams, they address it directly and candidly. You might have worked with leaders who think that conflicts, just like the economy, will work themselves out and the problems will eventually disappear. This is false, and only shows their flaw in this department. It takes a lot of courage to address problems, resolve conflicts, and ensure that everyone is held accountable.

The Six Styles of Leadership

According to Daniel Goleman, there are six styles of leadership, which is extraction from research done on 3,871 executives. They are:

- Visionary: Get people to take action toward a vision, best implemented when a change is needed or when there is a clear direction. This is the best climate you want to bring to the workplace.

- Coaching: Develop people so they can perform their job better, best implemented when helping people and building long-term strength. This is a positive style of leadership.

- Affiliative: Create emotional harmony and bonds, best implemented to heal emotional wounds after conflicts or to motivate people in stressful situations. This is a positive style of leadership.

- Democratic: Establish consensus through participation, as the name suggests, best implemented to get as much input as possible or to create consensus. This is a positive style of leadership.

- Pacesetting: Expect flawless work, excellent performance, and self-direction, best implemented to get quick results from a highly competent and skilled team. This is a negative style of leadership if used for an extended period of time without combining it with any of the above styles.

- Commanding: Possibly the worst style of leadership, it involves demanding immediate compliance but it works best in crisis or with problematic people.

Of course, all leaders do not use any specific styles at all times. Each of them fit different situations and a good leader should know how to change between them when the context requires it. Moreover, each of these styles relates to emotional intelligence.

How to Improve

If you lack any of the nine qualities, do not despair. There are plenty of ways to improve yourself and harness the power of emotion.

Encouraging Enthusiasm

Start by speaking with a smile on your face, holding a good posture, animation, force, gesture, and having a brisk pace. Use upbeat and positive language. Focus on opportunities and possibilities than challenges or problems. Express your personal optimism and excitement about the topic at hand. Never be too afraid of celebrating when the group is successful. Finally, provide extensive positive feedback and minimize negative messages. Of course, negative messages are inevitable, but try to maintain a ratio of 5 positive to 1 negative or corrective message.

Having a Vision

Describe your vision of an ideal future state or condition using specific and vivid terms. Talk with individual employees and ask about how they work enhances the overall strategy of the organization. Give them a better picture of what they do by connecting what they do to the fulfillment of the customer needs and proving a better service in the organization. When you initiate new programs, procedures, or project, push to extend the time horizon. Give your employees a picture of the impact of these programs, procedures, or project by telling them how they influence the company or business a few years from now. Finally, give meaning to their work by emphasizing the meaningfulness of their work and its impact on customers.

Encourage Involvement

Make your employees feel supported and involved by seeking the opinions of all group members on important strategic decisions. Emphasize the positive elements of any new suggestion before raising any concerns. Specifically, ask about each individual's career aspirations. Ask about their ideal work assignments and what they think they can contribute in addition to what they do. Provide development opportunities for everyone as well as supportive messages to the team. Link the work of the team to values that each individual worker cherishes. Reward their efforts and contribution, not only achievement. Set up regular meetings with direct reports and minimize interruptions and distractions. A good leader also expresses their heartfelt appreciation for the group's contribution and reward collaboration and cooperation while discouraging competition within the team and with other teams.

Being an Expert

This part is pretty straightforward. Remain up-to-date with the latest technology and research that is related to your work. Share that information freely so your employees can be up to date as well. To do that, take the time to share your technical information with other members of your organization. Volunteer information that could help others, and never withhold any useful data. Bring in outside experts to educate you and your group if you must. Finally, encourage innovative solutions to your problems.

Be Principled

Put your core beliefs and values on paper and share it with members of your team. Take the time to write down commitments and promises made to individuals and review them periodically to ensure that they are being honored. When you can, invite feedback from colleagues regarding any areas where your behavior is not aligned with the values. Encourage your employees to speak up if they think that the organization is cutting corners. Weight in on the side of compassion and tolerance when you can.

Be the Driver

Meet all personal commitments on time and with high quality. Follow through with others on the dates when items are to be delivered or projects completed. Meet with team members to deliberately raise the bar of performance via a stretch goal. Encourage employees of your team to escalate their pace with the knowledge that speed clears away barnacles off the boat's hull. Finally, hold people accountable for continuous improvement.

The Five Components of EI in Leadership

Previously, we mentioned how self-awareness, self-regulation, motivation, empathy, and social skills are key elements of emotional intelligence. The more you manage each of these areas as a leader, the better a leader you will be. Here are some ways you can improve in those departments.

Self-Awareness

Keeping a journal is a good idea as it helps you improve your self-awareness by writing down your own thoughts. That way, you can return to your journal and look at what you have written, therefore observing yourself from a third-person perspective.

Slowing down helps when you are experiencing anger or other strong emotions. Take the time to examine why instead of making decisions in a snap. Remember that, no matter what happens, you are the one who chooses how to react to it.

Getting out of the comfort zone does put you in an uncomfortable position, but it makes you more aware of your own feelings. Instead of bottling them up, focus on those emotions and go through them. Plus, if you have identified the border of your comfort zone, you know where you can improve, so take the time to wander out of it to achieve personal growth.

You should also identify your triggers, which can be a person, situation, or condition that makes you emotional and cause you to do something. It could be a noisy environment that disrupts your concentration, or a demanding boss that drains your energy. The usual response would be to shut down, especially at work where emotional outbreaks are prohibited. Still, even if you try to hide your emotions, your body will give it all away anyway. Therefore, identifying your triggers can help you control the outcome as you know what kind of emotions to expect next so you can take proper action to control it. If you want to, you can go all the way and identify the reason behind the trigger, meaning you find out why something pushes your buttons. Maybe the noisy environment irritates you because you are better in writing and reading than talking and listening, or you hate your manager because he or she reminds you of a previous manager that used to abuse their power.

We all have a habit of judging our feelings and label them as positive or negative, which would make us lose the ability to regard and be aware of them. Here, bad feelings are identified as something that you should avoid at all costs, and you would feel ashamed of yourself if you have that feeling. On the other hand, good feelings are something that you feel should strive toward, but they can run wild and drain your energy. Never judge your feelings, because they are nothing more than just feelings. However, they do tell you a few things. If you feel happy, it is probably because you accomplished something. If you feel mournful, it is because you lost something. If you regard your emotion as is, you might be able to understand it and understand what your mind is trying to tell you.

Let's face it. We all have made decisions when we are in a bad mood at a certain point in our life. During those moments, you lose sight of the good things in your life and you suddenly hate everything. You could be frustrated with your family, where you are, or just dissatisfied with yourself. Of course, you know deep down that most of what you think is not really true, but you cannot really get rid of your thoughts. On the flip side, you should never decide or make promises when you are happy, either. It is very easy to do something that you would really regret later. Making you feel excited is the first thing skilled salesmen do to sell you things that you do not really need. When they offer you the merchandise then, you will overestimate the price and pay too much for it. This is not saying that good moods are bad or anything, but you should never make decisions when you are emotional, especially life-changing decisions.

Taking a step back and view yourself from a third-person view is a good strategy to improve your self-awareness as you can let go of your narrow, first-person view. Doing so allows you to be more aware of your emotions as they come to life with your thoughts. Try putting yourself between the triggers and your reaction so you can understand how they connect. For instance, if you are a parent of a young boy and you want to cook up something nice for him for dinner. You came up with a dish with vegetables and meat, and you put a lot of effort into making it, only to have your kid complain about how horrible the food tastes and spit it on the floor you just cleaned. Now, any parents would be angry, but if you take a step back, you might see yourself as a parent who is worried about the fact that their kid is not getting enough vitamins and should eat healthily.

Will Smith uploaded a view on YouTube, and he said that the key to life is running and reading and that there have been billions and billions of people out there and there is not a problem that has not been solved yet. What does that mean? In this context, it means that there is a wide range of emotions, but they are the same for every one of us. We are all unique, but what we feel is the same, so you should stop thinking that nobody understands you. Start looking for emotions in movies or music. If it moves you, then it says something about you. If you learn more about the character or meaning in the music, you might discover something about yourself. If you can relate to lyrics, then it could be important. Look up what the lyrics and see what they mean. This can help you find ways to express your emotions.

Another way to improve your self-awareness is by occasionally consulting your values and then act accordingly. Your life is always changing and demanding, so much so that you would often focus on external things. At one point, you will feel overwhelmed. If so, then it is time to stop and review your values. Are things going the way you want to? What about your jobs, your family? Put that against your value and see if they align. If not, find ways to steer things back so your values remain uncompromised.

Finally, remember that there is a blind spot in all of us. There is a part of us that only we know that hides our deepest, darkest secrets, then there is another part of us that is public. The blind spot is something that you do not see about yourself. After all, your view of yourself is never impartial. Others might see something that you do not. That is why you should never be afraid to look for outside help. Ask your family or friends for feedback. They are more than willing to point out a few flaws about yourself. While they do that, observe and listen with an open mind. Never get defensive because the people closest to you only want to help you improve.

Self-Regulation

Leaders who can manage their emotions effectively do not usually attack others verbally, make rushed or emotional decisions, stereotype people, or compromise their own values. Self-regulation is, after all, all about remaining in control. Self-regulation is also related to a leader's flexibility and commitment to personal accountability. There are a few ways to improve self-regulation.

First, know your own values. Do you know exactly what you will absolutely not compromise? What values are the most important to you? Take some time to examine your code of ethics. If you know what is most important to you, then you have something to refer to when you need to make a moral or ethical decision. You know you will make the right choice.

Moreover, hold yourself accountable. If you often blame others when something goes south, stop! Instead, look at yourself and admit your mistakes and face the consequences, whatever they are. Holding yourself accountable makes others trust you more because they know that you will not bail out on them when things go wrong. Your decisions will be more valued because they know that you have thought about the consequences you will face should things go awry. Plus, you will sleep better at night and you will also earn the respect of those around you.

Finally, when you are in a challenging situation, be very careful of how you act. If you are used to relieving your stress by shouting at someone else, then start practicing deep breaths to calm yourself down. Moreover, write down all of the negative things you want to say, rip it up, and throw it away. Abraham Lincoln once wrote a strongly-worded letter to Gen.,George G. Meade, blaming him for letting Robert E. Lee escape after Gettysburg which would otherwise end the civil war.But the letter was never sent out. George Meade had never seen the letter. Lincoln realized that criticizing someone is pretty much pointless because brutally chastising someone only makes them defensive, justifying their actions, hurting their pride and arouses resentment. At that time, the last thing Lincoln want is to make people under him feel divided. So, instead of criticizing someone openly and cause resentment, express your emotions on paper and destroy it along with your emotions. Plus, it helps you challenge your reactions to ensure that they are fair.

Motivation

Motivation means motivating yourself and others to push toward the goals, not to mention maintain a high standard for the quality of work. There are a few ways to improve motivation.

Start by reexamining why you are doing your job. It is really easy to forget what you really love about your career. Take some time out of your day to remember why you even applied for the job and stayed in for so long. If you are unhappy with your current role and you have problems thinking of why you wanted the job, use the 5 whys to discover your purpose. This is a simple technique to direct you to the root of a problem quickly.

First, gather people who are familiar with the problem. In this case, that means your coworker, friends, and family. Discuss it with the group and write a short, clear problem statement that everyone can agree on. Then, put the sentence on a large whiteboard.

Ask "Why?"

This is the one question that children ask very often, and you might already be tired of hearing it repeatedly. But this is the route to find your solution. For example, if you have problems meeting deadlines, ask why. It sounds simple, but you need to analyze the problem through and through to come up with reasonable answers, which is a great thing. The search for the answer is grounded in fact. It must be accounts of things that happened, not speculations of what might happen. That way, the 5 whys is a process of deductive reasoning. This can lead you chasing down hypothetical problems quickly, creating more confusion because you might generate a lot of possible causes. That is where your team comes in.

They might come up with the obvious answer, or many plausible ones. Put their answers, and yours, on the board as succinct phrases instead of single words of long statements.

Ask "Why?" a Few More Times

Working from the third step, ask three or four "whys" in succession. Put the question up each time after the answer to the previous question, and record your response again. Try to move quickly from one question to the next so you still have the full picture before you make any conclusions.

Know When to Stop

You know when you need to stop asking "why" when you have revealed the root cause, which happened after you can no longer elicit a useful response and you can no longer go any further. Then, the right counter-measure or process change should be evident.

It is also worth pointing out that the above guideline is just a rule of thumb. In some cases, you should ask a few more "Whys" just for good measure so you can really get to the root of the problem. Sometimes, you will reach your answer before your fifth "why". Basically, stop asking "why" when useful answers stop coming.

Moreover, when you go through your questions, you will find that someone did not take necessary actions. The great thing here is that it prompts you to go even further than just putting blame on others and ask why that happened. This line of questioning could lead you to organizational issues or areas where certain processes need to be improved.

If you found more than one reason in the third step, repeat the process in each reason until you found the root cause of each one of them.

Address the Root Cause(s)

When you have found at least one true root cause, you need to discuss with your team about what counter-measure to take to prevent the problem from occurring. Then, keep a close watch on how effective your countermeasures are. They might not be effective, so you will most likely be making changes to them or outright replace them with something different. If that happens, perhaps you should repeat the above process again to make sure you identify the right root cause.

Empathy

For leaders, managing a successful team solely relies on them having empathy. Leaders with empathy can understand what it feels like working under themselves by putting themselves in someone else's shoes. This can also mean that they help develop the people on their team by challenging others who act unfairly, give constructive feedback, and listen to those that need it. To earn respect and loyalty from your team, you need to prove that you are empathic to them. So, how can you work on empathy?

First, put yourself in someone else's position. This should be obvious, but many people overlook this step. No one understands your own point of view than yourself, after all. But instead of being defensive about it, take the time to look at situations from other's perspectives.

Pay attention to your body language, because your body speaks a lot more than your mouth. When you listen to someone, you might move your feet back and forth, cross your arm, bite your lip, tilt your head, etc. These little things tell others how you really feel about a situation, and the message you send out might be more negative than positive. By learning how to read body language, you can be a great leader because you can also understand how someone else really feels. So, you can respond appropriately.

Respond to your feelings. When you ask your assistant to work late, they might agree, but you can hear their disappointment. If that happens, respond to their feelings. Tell them that you appreciate their commitment to work the extra hours and that you would feel frustrated too if you are asked to work late. If applicable, think of some ways to compensate for the extra hours. For example, if you have asked someone to work late, give them Monday mornings off to compensate.

Social Skills

Leaders who perform well in the social skills department of EI can communicate very well. Such a leader can take both good and bad news, and they are very adept at getting people to be excited and enthusiastic about a new project.

With good social skills, leaders can also manage change and resolve conflict diplomatically. Such leaders are rarely satisfied with keeping the status quo, but they do not just sit at the sideline and let everyone else dot the hard work. They set an example with their own behavior. Here are some ways you can build your social skills.

Conflict Resolution

The most important thing a leader should know is how to resolve a conflict. Learning conflict resolution skills is critical if you want to be an effective leader. After all, conflict is inevitable when you work with others. People have different viewpoints and those differences can escalate into conflict under the right circumstances. How you handle conflict as a leader will ultimately decide if it works to the team's advantage or contributes to its demise.

Resolving conflict requires respect and patience. Our emotions, perceptions, and actions are all involved in the conflict, so we need to address all three to resolve it. The key here is to replace negative experiences with positive ones.

Preparation

First, start by acknowledging that the conflict exists and the fact that it needs to be addressed before it can be managed or resolved. The issue here is that people often ignore the first signs of conflict because they thought that it is trivial or that it is hard to discern between an actual conflict or a healthy debate that teams thrive on. If you are unsure, consult it with your team. When the whole team recognizes that it is a problem, the conflict resolution process can start. Then, discuss how the conflict impacts the team as a whole in terms of performance and team dynamics.

From there, agree to a cooperative process and communication. Everyone needs to agree to help in resolving the conflict. This involves putting the team first and setting aside your own opinions or ideas for the moment. IF someone wants to win more than to resolve the conflict, you might find yourself at a stalemate. Also, open communication is critical to conflict resolution. Everyone involved needs to talk about the problem and discuss their feelings. Here, you need to practice active listening, which we had discussed previously. This is because you need to understand where others are coming from to move on with the discussion.

Understanding the Situation

When everyone is ready to solve the problem, you need to understand what is going on. To do so, everyone needs to understand each other's point of view. Take the time to do so to ensure that everyone feels heard and understood. While all conflicts can be resolved logically, addressing the strong emotions behind all conflicts is just as important to reveal the true nature of the conflict. Here are some steps.

First, clarify each other's positions. Each position needs to be identified clearly whether there are obvious factions within the team that support a specific option, idea, or approach, or that everyone has their own unique view. This is extremely crucial as it helps the team see the facts more objectively with less emotion.

From there, list facts, beliefs, and assumptions underlying each position. Put up what each group or person believe, what they value, what facts or information they based their beliefs on, and what decision-making criteria and processes they used. Then, break the team into smaller groups based on the alliance. Analyze and dissect each position of these groups, assumptions, beliefs, and facts. Determine which are true and which are most important to the outcome. Identify additional, objective information that can be brought into the discussion to clarify points of uncertainty or contention. Ask yourself if additional analysis or evaluation is required.

When you consider the beliefs, assumptions, facts, and decision making that back up their positions, the group will understand each other's positions much better. This can reveal common grounds where everyone agrees on, not to mention revealing new ideas and solutions that is the best for the situation. As always, remain open to ideas rather than criticize or judge the perceptions and assumptions of others.

After the discussion, everyone should be much closer to reaching an agreement already. The process of uncovering facts and assumptions allow everyone to take a step back from their emotional attachments and see the problem more objectively. When you separate alliances, the flame of conflict can die out much quicker, and it is a lot easier to see the issue and facts laid bare.

Reach Agreement

Now that everyone understands each other's positions, the team needs to decide what decision or course of action to take. This is a lot easier because we already put all of the facts and assumptions on the table.

Should further analysis and evaluation is needed, agree on what needs to be done, by when and by whom, and so plan to reach an agreement in a set timescale. If applicable, define which decision making and evaluation tools to be employed.

Ifadditional work is needed, everyone needs to agree on the approach. Make sure that everyone is committed to working with the outcome of the proposed analysis and evaluation. Finally, make sure to take the time to celebrate and acknowledge the contribution everyone made toward reaching the solution. Doing so reinforces the team's cohesion and confidence in their problem-solving skills, and can help prevent further conflict.

Following this three-step process can help solve team conflicts efficiently and effectively. Basically, you need to understand each other's perspectives and use that to expand your own thoughts and beliefs on the issue.

Preventing Conflict

Of course, it is a lot easier if you prevent unhealthy conflicts from happening in the first place, in addition to solving them. There are a few key behaviors that everyone needs to work on to prevent conflicts:

- Immediately address the conflict instead of ignoring it
- Being open-minded: if someone has issues, they need to be expressed immediately to prevent them from festering
- Practice clear communication by articulating your thoughts and ideas clearly
- Practice active listening by paraphrasing, clarifying, and questioning
- Practice identifying assumption by asking yourself "why" on a regular basis
- Never let conflict get personal by sticking to the facts and issues, not personalities
- When looking for solutions, make sure that they are actionable. Focus on what can be changed.

- Encourage different points of view by insisting on honest dialogue and expressing feelings
- Never look to blame by encouraging ownership of the problem and solution
- Demonstrate respect by taking breaks and wait for emotions to subside if the situation escalates and negative emotions start bubbling up
- Keep team issues within the team because talking outside allows conflict to build up without being dealt with directly

Communication Skills

You also need to work on your communicating skill as well, which should be obvious from the start. Effective communication means that you can ask your subordinates to do something without insulting them, or misinterpretations. There are a few things you can do to improve your communication skills.

The Communication Process

First, you need to understand the process. Basically, there are four (or six, depending on how you see it) steps in the communication process. You encode a message, transmits it through a channel to the receiver, who then decodes the message and sends feedback to the source (you).

When you are aware of the proper process of communication, you can become more aware of your role in it, and able to identify what you need to do to communicate effectively, anticipate problems before they occur, and improve your ability to communicate as a whole.

Planning Your Message

First, you need to plan what you want to say, and why. Most of the time, people just go on and on, wasting both the speaker and the listener's time. So, identify why you are communicating, with who are you communicating, what they need to know, how you will send the message, and seek feedback on how well was your message received.

A good communicator uses the KISS (Keep It Simple and Straightforward) principle. Basically, you need to break down detailed, technical content into simple language that can be understood by anyone, with clear explanation. There are a few ways to accomplish this.

First, deconstruct the large message. Break it down to the bare ideas, the basic elements. Then, simplify the premise by taking out unnecessary information that does not contribute directly to the value expected by the listener. Using that value as a guideline, reconstruct your message from the simplified premise and communicate that in a language that is accessible to the wider audience. Use clear language, avoid the use of slangs or other acronyms that only a small number of people would understand. Einstein once said that if you can't explain something to asixyear-old, you don't understand it yourself. In short, communicate like you would with a sixyear-old (not literally, of course).

Creating Your Message

Next, you need to decide exactly how you want to say it. You are responsible for sending a clear and concise message. To do that, you need to consider how the recipient will perceive the message in addition to what you will say.

Most of the time, we focus on the message that we want to send and the way we want to send it, without really considering the recipient's perspective, which could lead to the loss of information as the recipient will not be able to receive the message properly.

To craft your message, focus on what you really need and want to say. From there, anticipate other people's reaction to your message. That way, you can choose the words and body language that allow other people to really hear what you are saying.

If you use written communication, ensure that the message is perceived as intended. This is because texts are as emotionless as they come unless you add emoji or write creatively. When writing, review your style, avoid slang, and familiarize yourself with your company's writing policies or style guides. Moreover, proofread your message for grammar and punctuation errors in addition to the tone, attitude, nuance, and other subtleties in your text. If you think that your message might be misunderstood, take no chance and clarify things immediately.

Finding the Right Channel

You also need to choose the best communication channel through which to send your message. You are looking for an efficient way to send your message while making the most of your communication opportunity.

While sending emails is practical for simple directions, it is not enough if you want to delegate a complex task. If that is the case, arrange a time to speak in person. Moreover, if you need to convey a message with negative emotional content, make sure that you communicate face to face. At the very least, communicate by phone so you can judge the impact of your words and alter your message correctly.

When selecting the best channel for your message, consider the sensitivity and emotional content of the subject, how easy it is to communicate detail, the receiver's preferences, time constraints, and the need to ask and answer questions.

Receiving and Interpreting a Message

We want to get our points out there, so we tend to focus on only the speaking bit as we have a lot of things to say. However, communication is a two-way street. You need to let the other person talk, and listen.

That does not mean that you should just stand there, nod your head off, and then forgot what they said a moment ago. Listening is a lot harder than you think. You need to practice active listening by looking at the person, paying attention to their body language, avoidingdistractions, nodding and smiling to acknowledge points, think back of what the person has said occasionally, allow them to speak without thinking what you will say next, and never interrupt them while they are speaking.

Empathic listening is also useful when you need to decide messages accurately. After all, you need to understand the emotions and underlying feelings behind the message so you can understand what they are actually trying to tell you. An example is when someone says that they're fine when they clearly are not. This is why understand body language is important.

Receiving Feedback

Without feedback, you can never be sure that the listener has understood your message. Feedback can be verbal or nonverbal. Feedback through body language is useful when you need to assess the impact of your message. You can see their defensiveness, agreement, level of interest, engagement, truthfulness, and more just by watching their facial expressions, gestures, and postures.

Of course, this goes both ways as well. As a speaker, understanding the listener's body language gives you an idea of what they are thinking so you can adjust your message appropriately to make it more understandable, appealing, or interesting. As a listener, you can read their body language to understand what they are actually trying to say. From there, you can ask questions to ensure that you have understood each other. That way, miscommunication can be avoided before it can do any harm.

If you are talking about something really important, it is always worth asking questions to make sure that both sides understand each other fully. The best way to check if you have understood what you heard is by putting the message in your own words and confirm whether it is what the speaker wants to say.

Giving Praise

As a leader, you can also inspire the loyalty of your subordinates just by giving them praise when they earn it. This skill is an art that is worth the effort.

As a Chinese philosopher Lao-Tzu once said, "To see things in the seed, that is genius." We now refer to this as appreciative intelligence, which is a term coined by TojoThatchenkery. Appreciative intelligence is the capacity of certain individuals to see the positive inherent potential of situations or people. To put it simply, it is the ability to see the future value in someone or something that is not readily visible in the present, be it a breakthrough product, top talent, or valuable solution. It is the ability to see the tall and mighty oak in an acorn.

The term originated from an author who studied the explosive entrepreneurial growth in Silicon Valley in the late 90s. Basically, appreciative intelligence partly fueled many highly talented immigrants across the glove to convene in the area and flourish. Here, the author noted that venture capitalists looking to fund the right ideas asked "How can I make this work?" instead of "What are the chances this idea will fail?" Doing so create an environment of high anticipation of positive results that became very contagious. It sparked a fever of opportunity, achievement, resilience, and possibility recognition.

Here, appreciative intelligence is the mental capacity of an individual who can reframe situations and have a keen eye for spotting what is really valuable and positive in a situation or people. Think of it as the glass half full or half empty situation. These individuals go a step further by envisioning how the positive aspect of that situation can be utilized to create a better future. For our glass half full/empty situation, these individuals see that there is more room for growth (the glass can hold more water) instead of seeing the lack of content. Having these two abilities in an organization, such as a leader who has high appreciative intelligence and uses appreciative inquiry approach (not to be confused with appreciative approach; the latter is an approach and methodology for analyzing organizations), constitutes a very powerful force to push forward positive change and inspire others to do their very best. Imagine how profound, healthy impact this would have on an organization's culture if leaders proactively and mindfully practice appreciative intelligence.

This kind of culture will fuel employees' motivation. Numerous surveys of what employees want consistently put "appreciation for work well done" way higher than "good wages". Ironically, managers surveyed put the latter above the former. Other surveys showed that the lack of praise, recognition, or appreciation is one of the reasons why employees leave companies.

Many leaders struggle when it comes to building trust in the organization. According to a study on trust in the workplace by Adele Lynn from the Lunn Leadership Group LLC, 54% of respondents said they would work for less remuneration if four trust-building factors were present. They are:

- Importance, which gives people a sense of the importance of who they are and the role they play in the organization.
- Touch: the connection with the leader, the feeling that the leader really cares about them
- Gratitude: being appreciated for their sacrifices and contributions through receiving genuine gratitude
- Fairness: the knowledge that leaders ensure equal and fair distribution of rewards.

One way to create all four trust factors is through recognition and praise. We feel an inner glow when we get a genuine compliment for a work that we put our heart into. It is the magic that just makes us smile without fail and go the extra mile for the person that gave us a sincere compliment. This is just how we are wired. If we do not feel this sensation, then awards, plaques, medals, appreciative notes,and emails or other tokens of appreciation or recognition would not worth a penny.

Many basic management courses will point out the importance of praising employees for their contributions. Even so, many well-meaning and caring leaders are still reluctant to show their appreciation of others' talents and contributions. Most of the time, such behavior is not their fault. Sometimes, those leaders grew up in an environment (in a family, for example) where praising is not common. Growing in such an environment would teach us to withhold praise, which is a behavior that we all need to uproot if we want to bring the best out of our employees. However, giving up such a habit will be difficult, if not nigh impossible. Many people feel embarrassed when they have to praise someone. So, how do you practice giving genuine compliments?

First, analyze the root cause of your problem. For example, if you are afraid of embarrassing others, remember that voicing out your compliments out loud in the public is not the only way to praise someone. Even the most introverted individual appreciates an email listing all their contributions to all staff. If you do not know how to do it, then read on and consider getting a coach for a few sessions to practice this key element of leader communication skill.

Sometimes, you withheld compliments just because you do not have enough time. Or so you think. While it is undeniable that leaders are often required to handle an increasing amount of problems during the day, you have more time than you think. It takes less than 10 seconds to tell someone, "This is an exceptional report. I appreciate the effort you put into this. Thank you," No matter how busy you are, take that 10 seconds to show that you care about your employee before moving on to do anything else. This is because every praise has its own "best before" date. Never delay its expression or put off complimenting until performance review time. If you see something praise-worthy, do so as soon as possible.

One problem that many leaders face here is giving a generic compliment. If anything, this is worse than not giving any at all. Make sure to make your genuine compliment memorably by being specific about the achievement. Many people would overlook a short "job well done", but "this was a pure genius", "I never thought of that", or "I would have missed this if you hadn't pointed it out" would be very memorable indeed.

Genuine praise does not need to be long and elaborate, either. It just needs to be genuine.

Finally, when you decide to drop by and deliver praise, never follow it up with a conversation about other projects or business matters. Just drop in, deliver the praise, and leave. That way, the recipient has more time to appreciate the moment of honor and gives the praise better value. You can always come back later for discussions on other problems.

Conclusion

This is pretty much everything you need to know in order to have a high degree of emotional intelligence. We hope that you find this book helpful in your endeavor to become a person upon whom others can trust and depend on. Taking upon such a role may not seem that big of a deal, but you will realize just how valuable a dependable individual is in the workplace or at home. Everything starts from having high EQ, and with it, you can succeed. Of course, that does not mean that you can become a CEO by just having high EI alone. IQ and technical skills matter, but EI will be key to success. Technical skills and IQ are easier to improve upon than EQ, and you will find that you need to work on the latter more than you think. May the path ahead of you be challenging yet rewarding, and may luck smiles upon you.

Printed in the USA
CPSIA information can be obtained
at www.ICGtesting.com
LVHW010414150823
755264LV00005B/442